Legacies

Legacies

INTERVIEWS WITH MASTERS OF PHOTOGRAPHY
FROM *DARKROOM PHOTOGRAPHY* MAGAZINE

Janis Bultman

The photographs in this book are reproduced by permission and courtesy of the following:
Lou Stoumen, Lee D. Witkin, André Kertész, Pete Turner, Mary Ellen Mark, and Robert
Mapplethorpe: Kurt Fishback. Ruth Orkin: Courtesy of Mary Engel. Ray K. Metzker: Estate
of Ray K. Metzker. Courtesy of Laurence Miller Gallery. Aaron Siskind: Neal Rantoul. Barbara
Crane: © Chester Alamo-Costello. Bill Pierce: ©Eugene Pierce. Elliott Erwitt and Gordon Parks:
René du Carufel. Sonja Bullaty and Angelo Lomeo: Robert F. George. Alfred Eisenstaedt: The
Tony Spina Collection: Walter P. Reuther Library, Archives of Labor and Urban Affairs, Wayne
State University. Ernst Haas: Mark Harmel. Roman Vishniac: Andrew A. Skolnick/Wikimedia
Commons/Public Domain.

ISBN-13: 9780692834435
ISBN-10: 0692834435
Library of Congress Control Number: 2018933928
Quercus Agrifolia Press, Coralville, IA

Published by Quercus Agrifolia Press

To my parents, Wayne and Madelon Bultman,
and my children, Jennifer and Laura Levy

Acknowledgments

Thank you to the Masters of Photography who opened their homes and studios to me and gave so generously of their time and stories.

Special thanks to the extraordinary Ken Werner for his singular vision and unflagging generosity over the years.

Thank you to my dear friends and former colleagues Kimberly Torgerson and Christine Hebner Richardson for much good work and many good times. Thank you to Shantam Sheptow, Susan R. Keller and everyone at Sheptow Publishing and *Darkroom Photography* magazine, without whom these interviews—and this book—would not have been possible.

Thank you to the photographers whose portraits grace these pages: Chester Alamo-Costello, René de Carufel, Morris Engel, Kurt Fishback, Robert F. George, Mark Harmel, Eugene Pierce, Neal Rantoul, Andrew A. Skolnick, Tony Spina, and to the following for their indispensable help in obtaining them: Mary Engel, Laurence Miller, the Walter P. Reuther Library at Wayne State University, and the Creative Commons.

Thank you to my intrepid team of readers, critics, and cheerleaders: my daughters, Jennifer Levy and Laura Levy; my sister, Carol Escajeda; and dear friend and kindred spirit Jeanne Shoemaker.

Most especially, thank you to my husband, Gary Reimer—for everything.

Contents

Acknowledgments ·vii

Foreword · xiii

Introduction· ·xv

Herbert Bayer (1900-1985)
Many Paths from the Bauhaus · 1

Lou Stoumen (1917–1991)
Converging Forces · 11

Lee D. Witkin (1935–1984)
A Candid Chat· 23

Ruth Orkin (1921–1985)
Candor and Candids · 37

Ray K. Metzker (1931–2014)
A Formalist with Heart· 47

Val Telberg (1910–1995)
Unsettling Dreams · 57

André Kertész (1894–1985)
An Up and Down Life · 63

Aaron Siskind (1903–1991)
Conflicting Rhythms · 73

Barbara Crane (1928–)
Fresh Angles · 85

Bill Pierce (1935–)
Ticket to Danger · 95

Elliott Erwitt (1928–)
A Wry Eye · 107

Gordon Parks (1912–2007)
Fighter with a Camera · 119

Sonja Bullaty (1923–2000) and Angelo Lomeo (1921–)
Double Visions· 131

Pete Turner (1931–2017)
The Turner Touch · 143

Alfred Eisenstaedt (1898–1995)
The Affable Observer · 153

Ernst Haas (1921–1986)
A Conversation · 163

Roman Vishniac (1897–1990)
A People Remembered · 173

Mary Ellen Mark (1940–2015)
Street Shooter· 185

James J. Kriegsmann (1909–1994)
An Eye for Entertainers · 195

Robert Mapplethorpe (1946–1989)
Bad Boy Makes Good· 203

About the Author· 209

Foreword

Cameras don't take photographs; people do.

When I created the editorial plan for *Darkroom Photography* in the late 1970s, the magazine was intended, of necessity, as a commercial endeavor. My goal was to share—or steal—as many as possible of the subscribers and advertisers of the large, generalist photography magazines of the day.

Those magazines, with names like *Popular Photography*, *Modern Photography*, and *Petersen's Photographic*, were very technically oriented, and hardware, especially new cameras produced by their big advertisers, received a nearly fetishistic degree of attention. In contrast, serious photography—and the photographers who created it—was treated almost as an afterthought. And even those pages devoted to imagery tended to be dominated by slick, commercial color photographers like Jay Maisel and Pete Turner.

As a serious, art-oriented photographer myself, I wanted to feature as much creative, artistic photography as possible. While much of the magazine's content was designed to offer its readers "perceived utility"—tips, tricks, and techniques coupled with detailed darkroom hardware and materials coverage—thanks to its rapid success (zero to one hundred thousand subscribers in two years), I was increasingly able to devote a substantial number of its pages to great photography.

The serious, long-form magazine interview was in its heyday back then—think the *Playboy* interview and Andy Warhol's *Interview* magazine. So it was natural for me to enlist that format and to try to feature famous, mature, photographic artists: people with experience and insight to share, along with stunning photographs. And so a major, regular feature of the magazine was born: Masters of Photography.

The only problem was to entice these increasingly famous artists to grant an interview to and share their images with a largely technical, information-driven niche magazine like *Darkroom*. The problem was compounded by the fact that I wasn't in a position to offer much financial compensation in return. What I *could* offer them, though, was an opportunity to speak freely about their work, their life, and the art of photography in general.

Crucial to the entire enterprise were a small group of skilled interviewers—people who could communicate on the same level as these highly intelligent, often-opinionated and sometimes difficult-to-deal-with stars of the photo world.

Enter Janis Bultman, who quickly became my go-to interviewer, my first choice for almost every project. Janis was hardly an expert in photography; when I first asked her to do a portrait of the legendary photo-artist Herbert Bayer, she was so nervous she couldn't hold the camera steady enough to take a suitable image. (I never asked her to take a portrait again.)

But Janis more than made up for it with her skills as an interviewer, her understanding of the creative process, and her empathy and energetic charm. And as the number of her published interviews reached critical mass, she was able to use them as "samples" to entice even more famous—and sometimes reclusive—photographers to grant her an interview. Sometimes I'd throw out a name—someone I honestly thought wouldn't say yes—and voilà, Janis had gotten the interview.

The remarkable and fascinating results of Janis's efforts are on display in the following pages. Aside from their intrinsic interest, they represent a kind of time capsule, a composite portrait of serious photography in the 1980s and early 1990s. The world of photography in general, and art photography in particular, has changed a lot since then, perhaps not for the better. But here, preserved in the crystalline amber of Janis's thoughtful interviews, is a broad yet deep view of that once-upon-a-time world. Read, learn, think, and enjoy.

Ken Werner
Sydney, Australia
January 2016

Introduction

From 1979 until 1988, I worked for *Darkroom Photography* magazine, initially as an editorial assistant in its San Francisco offices and later as a freelance contributing editor in Los Angeles and New York City. During that time, I interviewed twenty-one of the world's best and most influential photographers for the magazine's Masters of Photography series. Those interviews are reproduced here.

Darkroom Photography was the second of two commercial "niche" magazines launched by Paul Sheptow, a Wharton MBA who hailed from Ohio. The first was *Super-8 Filmaker*, in 1975. (The misspelling of its name is intentional. The thinking was that it made for a cleaner logo.) Sheptow, who counted filmmaking among his avocations, noticed there were no magazines for serious amateurs like himself, so he formed Sheptow Publishing and started one—in his living room, on the proverbial shoestring.

Super-8 Filmaker was a hit, and soon after, Sheptow moved his operation to San Francisco and identified another untapped niche: amateur darkroom enthusiasts. He contacted Ken Werner, a New York–based photographer and writer who was a nationally recognized authority on photographic technique. "He said, 'I've been successful serving the amateur-filmmaker niche,'" Werner remembers, "'And there are more darkroom enthusiasts than there are amateur filmmakers, so this could be big.'"

Werner was intrigued. He thought Sheptow might be on to something. And he had exactly the right background for what Sheptow had in mind. Werner's father was an amateur photographer and astronomer, so Werner had grown up in a house strewn with enthusiast magazines such as *Camera* and *Sky and Telescope.* "I developed an emotional affinity for them," he says.

Werner accepted Sheptow's challenge to create a template for a magazine for amateur darkroom enthusiasts. *Darkroom Photography: The Magazine for Creative Photographers* was launched with the January/February 1979 issue and quickly acquired a readership of one hundred thousand. Published eight times yearly, it was aimed at serious hobbyists, art photographers, and working professionals. It showcased outstanding creative photography, covered dark-room devices and gadgets, and provided technical information and business advice—like how to copyright photographs, the subject of my first published article. It also featured personalities—short takes on up-and-comers called Hot Shots as well as feature-length interviews with star photographers including Ansel Adams, Brett Weston, Lisette Model, and Judy Dater. The last page, called Final Frame, brought scores of over-the-transom submissions and years later was described by one successful submitter as "the most prestigious place in creative photography at the time."

I was hired in mid-1979, fresh out of college. Every day for almost a year, I boarded the F bus in Berkeley, traversed the Bay Bridge, disembarked at the TransBay Terminal, and walked the few blocks to Sheptow Publishing, which occupied the entire second floor of a squat building in the seedy Mission District. (Later it moved to a more respectable address at One Hallidie Plaza.) At the time, it was just one of two companies publishing national magazines in San Francisco. Mother Jones was the other. I was over the moon. As an English major who'd spent all her spare time taking classes in modern dance, I was extraordinarily lucky to get a job at Sheptow Publishing, but love trumped good sense, and I quit a year later to move to Los Angeles with my grad-school-bound boyfriend. My luck held, though—at least, career-wise. No sooner had I settled into our Venice apartment than Werner, now Editorial Director, called to ask me to interview Herbert Bayer, who was living in Montecito, near Santa Barbara. When I moved to New York City the following year, Werner kept calling with more assignments.

The Masters of Photography whom I interviewed in those years represent a cross-section of the profession in the predigital era. They include photojournalists like Alfred Eisenstaedt, Bill Pierce, and Gordon Parks; studio photographers like James J. Kriegsmann, Pete Turner, and Robert Mapplethorpe; experimenters like Herbert Bayer, Val Telberg, and Lou

Stoumen; landscape photographers like Sonja Bullaty and Angelo Lomeo; teachers like Ray K. Metzker, Aaron Siskind, and Barbara Crane; and two pioneering gallery owners, Lee D. Witkin and Laurence G. Miller (who represented Metzker and sat in on my interview with him). They had definite—and often conflicting—ideas about photography as well as the world in which they worked. They experimented. They pushed the boundaries of the medium. They risked their lives in war zones and gritty urban neighborhoods. They made art and celebrated sex, glamor, and rock and roll. They groused about editors, dealers, and each other. They were feted and cheated, endured poverty and obscurity, enjoyed fame and fortune—not always in that order.

When I interviewed them, I was a nervous, twenty-something kid. Initially, I knew nothing about either interviewing or photography. I learned as I went. I spent hours in museums, galleries, and libraries, studying photos, pouring over articles, and reading criticism. I made careful lists of what I would ask and what subjects I would cover.

I interviewed each photographer in person, at his or her home or studio. They were mostly eager to talk, perhaps because I was young and diffident and not the least bit intimidating. Some photographers were practiced interviewees who had their stories ready. I heard them out and solicited new ones. Others had to be coaxed and prodded. Some I had to interview more than once. Only one was snooty, a famous magazine photographer, whose assistants hovered throughout. His comments were so cryptic and condescending, *Darkroom* declined to publish his interview. But he was the lone exception.

Herbert Bayer was the consummate gentleman. André Kertész astonished me by insisting on taking me out to dinner to thank me for my time. Aaron Siskind was relaxed and gracious. Mary Ellen Marks was tense and restless. She liked our interview so much, she posted it on her website—without my permission. I didn't object. Ruth Orkin bristled when I suggested it might be dishonest to stage photojournalism, but we both agreed "American Girl in Italy" was a masterpiece of storytelling. Gordon Parks flirted. Lee Witkin was so likeable, I wanted him to be my new best friend. Robert Mapplethorpe was weak and barely articulate. He hadn't yet announced he had AIDS, which claimed his life two years later, but he was clearly ill. I left his studio, and I cried.

After each interview, I used a Dictaphone to transcribe my cassette tapes, first on an antique IBM typewriter and then on one of the first personal computers, an IBM Portable PC and dot matrix printer—gifts from my father who worked for IBM for forty years. The PC was big as a small suitcase and the envy of my on-again-off-again boyfriend, an editor at *Rolling Stone* who freelanced for *Penthouse* and borrowed my PC whenever he could. I lived hand to mouth in those days, barely able to make the rent on my East Village apartment, so I reused my tapes, taping over previous interviews, a decision I regret. I managed to preserve audio for only a handful of the interviews. At least I have the transcripts.

Meanwhile, back in San Francisco, things were in flux. In 1984, when Paul Sheptow turned forty, he sold Sheptow Publishing to Trailer Life Publishing (TLP), changed his name to Shantam, and retired to Northern California. The following year, Werner moved on. In 1987, photographer Jeff Dunas, who owned the Melrose Publishing Group, purchased the magazine from TLP and moved it to Los Angeles. In 1988, Dunas sold Melrose to Larry Flynt Publications (LFP), and *Darkroom Photography* joined LFP's stable of specialty magazines. In 1991, LFP changed the magazine's name to *Camera & Darkroom*. It ceased publication with the September 1995 issue.

By then, I too had moved on. My interview with Robert Mapplethorpe was my last for *Darkroom Photography.*

As mediums go, photography came late to the table. Just over two hundred years ago, Thomas Wedgewood discovered he could use sunlight and silver nitrate to print a transitory image. Shortly thereafter, the daguerreotype was born. Starting midcentury, daguerreotype cameras were deployed all over the world, and the profession of photography was launched with an explosion of black-and-white images of people, places, and things. Improvements came in quick succession, including smaller, cheaper cameras mass marketed to the public, still and moving-picture film, color photography, enlargers, flash photography, zoom and macro lenses, and more.

Fast-forward to 2016. Hardly anyone shoots film anymore. Photographers use digital cameras and edit their work on their computers, not in darkrooms. They talk about pixels, not grain. It's hard to imagine life without the camera. Everyone has one. We carry them in our pockets, photograph everything, and share instantaneously.

It wasn't always so, and in between then and now, these Masters of Photography made essential contributions to photography's meteoric ascendance as an art form, profession, and leisure activity. Their lives and work inspired and hastened what was to come. These interviews are their legacies, and certainly ours.

Janis Bultman
Coralville, Iowa
July 2016

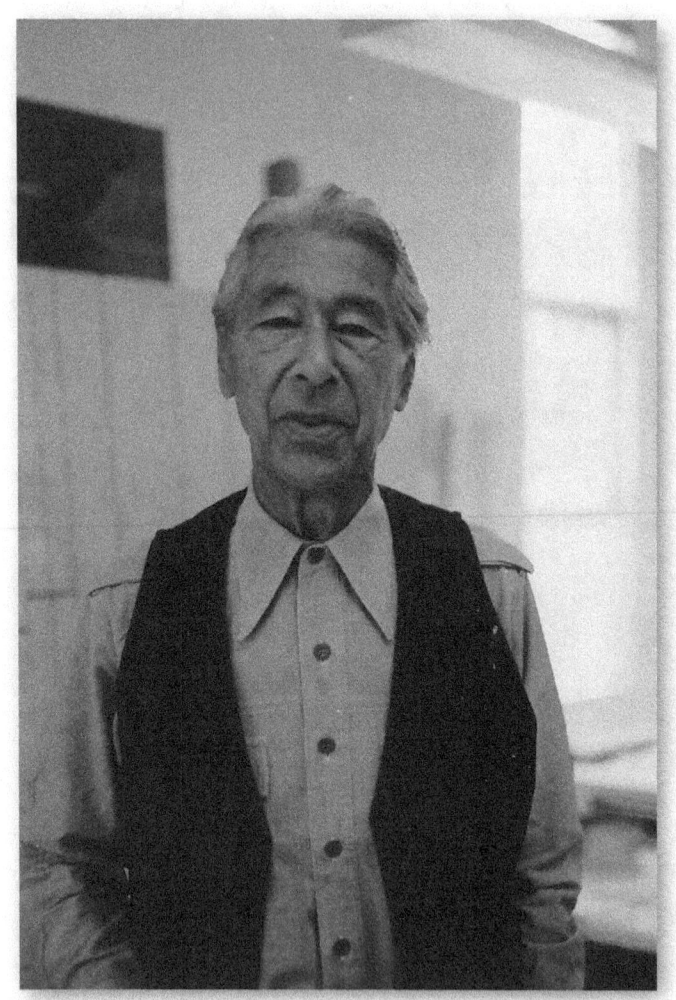

Photo by Janis Bultman

HERBERT BAYER (1900-1985)
Many Paths from the Bauhaus

Published January/February 1981

To call Herbert Bayer a versatile talent is almost an understatement. His repertoire of skills includes not only photography but painting, sculpture, architecture, typography, exhibition design, and the list goes on. He's authored several books on design and has won more prizes than he can modestly remember, including the German Photographic Society's coveted *Kulturpreis*.

A native of Austria, Bayer both studied and taught at Germany's famed Bauhaus. After relocating to America, he put the Bauhaus principles to work in Aspen, Colorado, where he was one of a group of artists, philosophers, and business people who designed its "total environment" and founded the Aspen Institute for Humanistic Studies. At eighty, Bayer isn't ready to retire. The latest addition to his already extensive resume is Art and Design Consultant for Atlantic Richfield Company.

Bayer had a hand in formulating many of the ideas about photography we now take for granted, and in the past few years, his photographs have been increasingly recognized not only for their craft but for their historical value. From his current home, a converted polo club in Montecito, California, Bayer shared his philosophies on art and artists, and reminisced about the early days of twentieth-century European photography.

JB: When did you start experimenting with photography?

HB: I got started in the early twenties while I was studying at the Bauhaus. We were working in many different media and I became interested in photography as a new and fascinating art medium. Several of us young people started experimenting with it. Then Moholy-Nagy joined the Bauhaus faculty in 1923, bringing with him his experiments with photograms. His wife, too, was a famous photographer. They excited and stimulated us.

JB: There was little interest in photography as an art form in Europe—except in certain circles—in the early twenties. But by 1929 Germany had become recognized as the birthplace of The New Photography. What was The New Photography?

HB: Well, the New Photography was really the discovery and use of new points of view. Like the bird's eye view or the frog's eye view—from above, below, from different perspectives.

JB: Your early camera images, then, are examples of the New Photography.

HB: Yes. I remember I once photographed a chair. It was only an object, but it was interesting. It had a life of its own. So I tried to photograph it in a new way that would bring out its character. I also photographed waves from above. It was different to look at waves this way.

I suppose the concept came partly from the Cubists' ideas of penetrating the subject or object to show it from all sides, then recombining it again to show a conglomerate of images. This sort of approach was in the air.

Science photography also began looking at new perspectives. It became possible to photograph microcosms and the stars. Of course, much has happened since then.

JB: Yet these years are now considered to be the formative years of contemporary photography.

HB: Yes…it was an exciting time. It was all new.

JB: What kind of equipment were you using then?

HB: This is always a question. In the beginning I only used cheap, small cameras with a fold-out bellows. They cost maybe 60 marks, which was then about $15. Now cameras are so expensive. Recently, I needed a new one, so I asked what a Hasselblad cost, and they told me close to $1,000. I ended up buying a 35mm Pentax to replace the one I had, which was getting old.

JB: But you would have preferred a larger format?

HB: I think 35mm is really a little small. It is such hard work for the printer. And you cannot get as sharp an image as you can with a larger format. My very early photographs, the camera images, were 4½ x 7½ cm. Later, I used 8 x 11½ cm. Then I switched to a 6 x 6 Rolleiflex. Today, I photograph mostly to make a record of my other work—for my slide file—so I use 35mm, but I like the square format for black-and-white. I'm planning to do more montages—I've always been interested in collage and montage—and I've collected some photos I want to use. I'd like to buy a larger format camera for this.

JB: How would you say the equipment you were using in the twenties compares with what's available now?

HB: It was primitive. I suppose there were better cameras on the market than mine, especially the large cameras professional photographers used. But they were of no use to me because I used the camera when I traveled, and I didn't want to carry a large camera with me.

JB: What about photo papers?

HB: Well, the old photographers, of course, used soft papers. They also used soft lenses because they wanted to get a painterly feeling.

JB: You're talking about photography prior to the New Photography, which was very impressionistic? When photographers were purposely blurring their images, copying what painters were doing at the time?

HB: Yes, and they sometimes altered their photos, covering up imperfections. So the papers were made for them, as well as the glass negative plates. Then this went out of fashion. Photographers wanted sharp, realistic images, so the industry complied and began making lenses and papers that would give a sharp image.

But this wasn't available at first and for many things, like my early posters and photomontages, I had to use images which weren't so sharp. People today don't understand that. The other day I met with a museum acquisition committee consisting of three photographers who were, if I may so say, unimportant photographers, little photographers. They were thinking of buying some of my photomontages. But my prints weren't sharp enough for them. They were not as technically perfect as you can make things today, and this was because of the times.

Also, we worked with glass negatives, and these have been rephotographed so they wouldn't have to be handled. Then, when I assembled my photomontages, I cup up other photos and rephotographed the final montage. Of course, the new image was not as sharp. But I didn't mind because this was a painterly concept. I sometimes chose grainy prints and rephotographed them purposely to get some grain.

JB: When you were at the Bauhaus, didn't you explore using photography in other applications, such as graphic design?

HB: Yes, I used it extensively in my graphic work. I had worked a great deal with typography for posters and the next step was to find illustrations that would work with the type. Photographs seemed the logical answer. You see, prior to that time posters were always painted, and I believed photography could be more effective because it was less subjective. It wouldn't show the personal character of a painting but would show the image as it actually is. The combination of photographs and type had a name: *typo-foto*. Then later, I turned to photomontage because it is much more pliable, and you can express more fantastic things—surreal things.

JB: What's the difference between your photomontages and what's known as your *fotoplastiken*?

HB: They are both montage forms, but I distinguish between the two. In photomontage, I cut up preexisting photos and reassemble them, pasting one on top of the other, sometimes retouching, and finally I photograph the result. This final photograph is the photomontage. It's a way of using objective photography to show more subjective ideas.

For my *fotoplastiken*, I set up an arrangement of objects in my studio, sometimes using string to prop them up. Then I photograph the setup. Later, I sometimes use an airbrush technique to touch out supporting props or add tiny clouds. Then this retouched photograph is photographed, and this is the *fotoplastiken*.

JB: You were one of the first to use photography in advertising. When did you start working with that?

HB: In 1928. But I don't like to call it advertising. It's graphic communication. We tried many new things. We experimented with display photography, hanging photos at angles, applying the idea of extended vision, instead of hanging them flat on the wall. I used this principle at the New York Museum of Modern Art when I designed the *Airways to Peace* exhibit in 1943. It was an exclusively photographic show. The photographs were suspended, but you could not see what was holding them up. There was no structure. I also used a ramp to raise visitors so I could use the floor space.

Another innovation I was involved with was the use of extremely large photos. We used them in exhibitions at trade fairs. This was partly because of the influence of the Constructivists in Russia, particularly Nisitsky. He used large, color photographs of political demonstrations at fairs in the provinces. The photos became large, color statistics for the purpose of instruction. I used the same principle at an exhibition for the Building Workers Union in Berlin in 1939.

JB: You're a firm believer in using photography in conjunction with something else, aren't you? A photo should be more than a pretty picture on a wall. It should instruct or communicate.

HB: Yes, my principle has always been that every project should have a purpose. It must do something—express or convey something. It's not simply an opportunity for the artist to do something artistic, although it has to be artistic too, within the given boundaries. It's like in architecture. You can't just make a fantasy. It has to stand up; the proportions have to be right. You have to consider your budget, the climate, what building materials are available, and so on. It's the ultimate function of the piece that rules the concept.

JB: All your exhibition prints are black-and-white. Have you worked much with color?

HB: No, I have not. I still feel, with all the progress, that color photography doesn't compare with what the eye registers. The colors are artificial, unnatural.

JB: Recently you've exhibited at the Arco Center for Visual Design and at the New York Museum of Modern Art. Where else have you shown your work?

HB: The Arco show has been traveling, and it will have its last showing in Aspen in January or February. In Europe, there is hardly a week that goes by when I don't receive some notice of an exhibition. There have been many in Germany, Switzerland, and Austria. Right now, I have an exhibit in my hometown of Linz, in Austria.

JB: Interest in your photographs seems to have really grown in the last few years.

HB: Well, in Europe the interest has been in the past ten to fifteen years, but here it's been in the past few years, yes.

JB: I'm afraid my politics are going to show in my next few questions. My editor cautioned me to be diplomatic, but I can't think of any other way to word this. You've worked for several large corporations—Container Corporation of America and Atlantic Richfield Company among them. Why did you choose to put your talents in the hands of these industry giants?

HB: Well, I first started working for Container Corporation not long after I came to America. They wanted me to design a corporate image for them. This was something new in America, and it interested me. I took charge of their advertising, designed the architecture of their offices, and handled anything that had to do with design.

JB: My generation has heard many times that you sometimes have to compromise your ideals if you work for a large, impersonal corporation. Did you have to make compromises?

HB: Well, this is always a question. When I first got started in New York, I had a difficult time. I was doing work for a few ad agencies. My ideas were more advanced than my clients' and concessions had to be made to their tastes. But at Container Corporation there were no compromises made to speak of because there was a very small committee that made all the decisions concerning design. It consisted of Mr. and Mrs. Paepcke—the president and his wife—and myself. None of the other executives were involved. And so I say it's always a question of how you come into a company. If you come in through the top, which I did through my friendship with Walter Paepcke, then you have power. I got into Atlantic Richfield Company the same way. I met the president when he bought my house in Aspen. He became active in the Aspen Institute for Humanistic Studies, in which I was also very active, and we became friends. He asked me to design a corporate image for him, and I've been working on that for the past three or four years.

JB: How did you get involved in the Aspen project?

HB: Walter Paepcke—the head of Container Corporation—was the one who really started what some have called the "Renaissance of Aspen." I was intrigued, and I moved there to help design it. It was here that the "Great Ideas of Western Man" advertising campaign germinated. It was the result of roundtable discussions at the Aspen Institute which Walter Paepcke founded. We chose quotations of some great man—a philosopher or statesman—and had an artist interpret it. Philosopher Monty Nadler, who was at the Institute at the time, helped us choose the quotations. Then various companies, including Container Corporation, sponsored the ads. This was something radical and revolutionary in advertising. When Walter Paepcke died and new executives took over, they didn't understand the campaign. They couldn't put their finger on how much money it was bringing in, because we didn't sell to the public, we sold to other companies. But the campaign put Container Corporation on the map. It gave it an internationally famous name.

JB: What do you do at Arco?

HB: I call myself consultant in Art and Design. I don't do the work myself. The Graphics Department in Los Angeles does that. I consult with various decoration or interior design firms. We work with various architects on the architecture, and so on. So I can operate from here.

JB: Then you're the "idea man."

HB: I'm the idea man and also curator and supervisor. I oversee each job. And I buy the corporation's art collection.

JB: One of the prime Bauhaus concerns was how to combine art with industry. For example, designing a piece of furniture that was not only beautiful but that could be mass produced. Do you think this philosophy has been one of the things that kept you close to industry?

HB: Well, yes. The Bauhaus philosophy and principles are in my bones. I believe in them. However, I've always been against the term "Bauhaus Style." A style is something immutable. It's not flexible. It implies no more growth. But principles can be interpreted in new and individual ways. My work has changed over the years—there are always new and different projects—but I always approach it the same way. I ask myself questions about function. Then I find an artistic solution.

JB: One of Walter Gropius's goals, when he founded the Bauhaus, was to teach students to become competent in many craft areas, which you've obviously done. Today it seems that most artists choose to specialize in one medium. Do you think this limits them?

HB: Yes, I do. Too many artists just sit in their studios, painting their thing, or go out and photograph, and then just wait around for somebody to like their work and buy it. They're only concerned with what's inside the picture frame. There's no connection to life outside the studio or beyond the photograph. In former times there was always a connecting link between what the artist did and everybody else. It was religion, or the state had to be glorified. There was always something to which the artist could orient himself, but now there's nothing. And with so many people wanting to become artists we will have, in fact we *already* have, a proletariat of very mediocre artists. I say they should turn their talents to something useful. I believe a well-designed, good-looking chair is more important than one more of millions of mediocre paintings or photographs.

JB: You've been a photographer, typographer, painter, writer, architect, and sculptor, to name a few. If you had to choose a label for yourself, what would it be?

HB: An artist. I think the new kind of artist has to be this way.

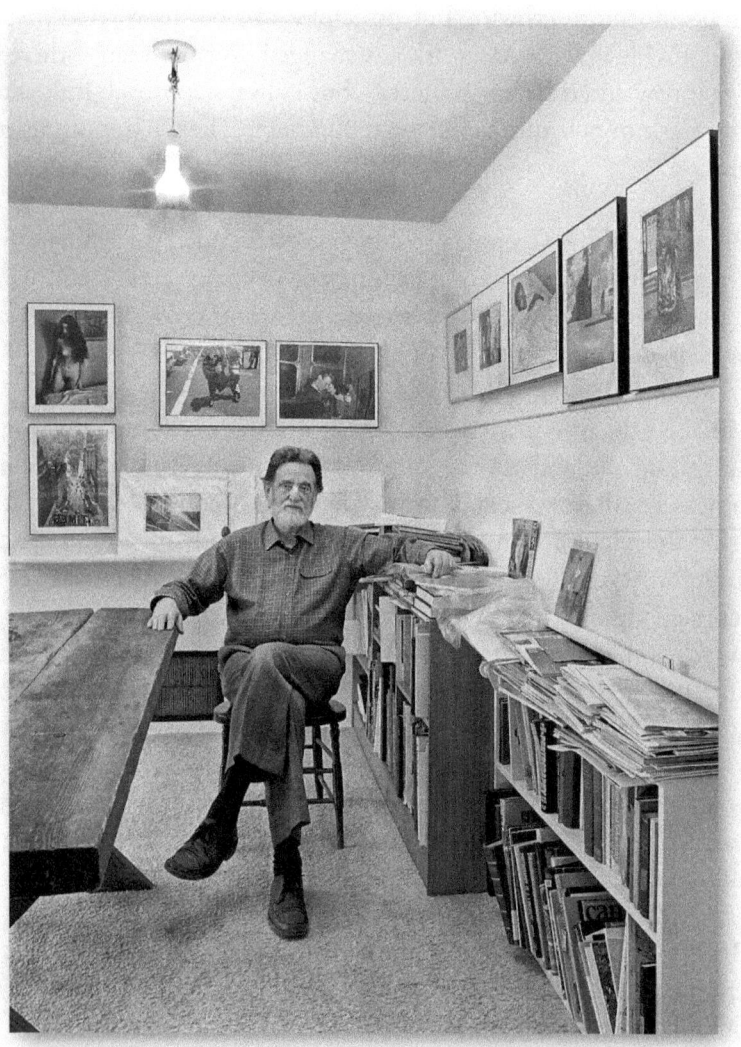

Photo by Kurt Fishback

Converging Forces

Published December 1981

Poet, street photographer, and Academy Award–winning filmmaker Lou Stoumen has never respected conventional boundaries between the arts. He smuggled still photography into filmmaking, collecting two Oscars in the process when he was the first to "animate" photographs in motion pictures. Lately, he's been defying border guards again, bringing filmmaking concepts to still photography. Stoumen often adds a third dimension to the traditionally two-dimensional photographic medium by adding a poetic written "soundtrack" to his still photographs. Audience reaction has typically been varied: photography purists dismiss his "paper movies" as eccentric mutations, while the less conservative praise them as "unique to the point of establishing a new form."

JB: When did you start making paper movies?

LS: As a boy. I made the first one when I was twenty, in 1939, and I've made five since. I've always worked with text and pictures—words and photographs.

JB: You've written that the paper movie's prototype is the "homely family photo album." Is the paper movie solely a book?

LS: Well, in its primary form it's a book, but it's nice to have it in a fast form, like an exhibit.

JB: When I looked through your most recent book, *Ordinary Miracles,* I was struck by the way the juxtaposition of photographs and text gives the viewer a kind of double treat. The photo catches the eye first, so you look at it and react to it. Then the text catches the eye and often gives the photo a whole new twist.

LS: I'm glad you appreciate that. There is a lot of resistance to putting words and pictures together, particularly from museum and gallery directors. Often, they'll give photographers a whole wall of photographs with a tiny little text block way over to the side. I don't like that. I like the relation between words and pictures. I think that's the way the mind works. We're verbal, and we're visual.

JB: When you exhibit your paper movie photographs, does the text accompany them?

LS: If I have anything to say about it, yes.

JB: Why would an exhibitor object to including the text?

LS: Well, they have this pure attitude—and I respect it, it's one way to go—that the photograph has to do it all. Indeed, a photograph does have a great power all by itself. It's an object of contemplation, meditation. But so often a photograph by itself has a way of just sitting there. I like the additional dimension my writing—anybody's writing—gives a photograph.

JB: In *Ordinary Miracles* you often write about why you took a certain photograph, so that the viewer can draw on not only on his or her own personality in reacting to the photo but the photographer's as well.

LS: Yes, and that's what these museum people object to. They feel the photographer's personality should be irrelevant. I think a lot of current exhibition practices are kind of snotty and elitist in that respect.

JB: What was your first paper movie like?

LS: I'll show it to you, but I'd prefer you didn't read it. It's a long narrative, political/sensual thing. My first, sort of, statement. I don't know that it's poetry. It's really juvenilia. I kept text and photographs in separate sections.

JB: Why did you keep them separate?

LS: I didn't yet have a hold of the paper movie form where text and photographs interact. I made the second during World War II. I was in the army, in India, Burma, and China, working on the army magazine, *Yank*. I saw that a lot of good photography was being done and thought, why not turn it into a book? So I put together *Yank's Magic Carpet*. We printed twenty-five thousand and they sold out instantly in the PX [Post Exchange]. We went through three more editions—a total of about one hundred thousand copies. One-third to one-half the photographs and all the text are mine. It's really a book for homesick GIs.

JB: How does a paper movie usually evolve? Do you do the photography first, then write the soundtrack, or vice versa?

LS: It has always taken me years to do a book. I stew about it and work on it on and off. In contrast, my latest project has been a remarkable experience. Including the photography, it's all been done in the past six months. It just came on me in a rush. To answer your question by its example, I didn't set out to do a book at all. I simply began doing a different kind of photography with a smaller camera. The body of work grew out of my concerns about ecology and nuclear weapons, and there seemed to be a unity to it. I suddenly said to myself, "Hey! This is a book!" Then I began writing text. I'd already taken three-fourths of the photographs. As the book's form evolved, I discovered I wanted a photograph of this and a photograph of that, so I went out and made them.

JB: You mentioned that you started using a different camera. What kind?

LS: Up until recently I've always used a larger format camera. There are only two 35mm images in *Ordinary Miracles.* Then the little Olympus XA came into my life. I really got it for making visual notes, because it's so compact, and I can take it everywhere I go so easily. You can literally carry it in your breast pocket.

I was amazed by the image quality. It's not quite as sharp as bigger 35mm cameras and lenses, and the lens has a property of vignetting the corners of the print a bit. I don't think it will give elegant 16 x 20 prints, although here I'm guessing. I haven't tried that yet. But I took all the photographs for the new book with it, including the cover photograph, which is now one of my favorites. The nice thing about the camera is people don't take me seriously when I'm shooting with it.

JB: That brings us to the subject of street photography. In the essay printed at the back of *Ordinary Miracles,* you write, "I am a street photographer and have from boyhood obsessively photographed the people, events, and light of everyday life." In your experience, what is it about a given scene that makes it a street photographer's subject?

LS: There are certain things that are interesting—relationships between people, anger, and love. That's what interests me—people in the context of the world, which is usually on the street. I've done very little studio photography because I don't like to set things up. There are certain moments of unrehearsed human life that I feel very passionate about. It's instant recognition. You sort of smell it. It's really instant choreography. As a photographer, I orchestrate and organize it all into a photograph.

JB: Do you take a number of shots of such a situation, or do you wait until just the right image is there?

LS: I shoot a little bit more freely now than I used to. I used to use a larger camera, for one thing, and it wasn't as convenient to take several shots. But on certain photographs you only get one chance. Take "The Butcher." The man just emerged. A second after the exposure, he saw me, and the moment changed. In street photography, observation often changes the object being observed, which is why it's often necessary, as in this photograph, to work very fast. You have to get to know your camera so well that you can use it automatically, without spending a lot of time determining exposure, focus, and whatnot.

In the street, you do all your creative work by recognizing the symptoms of a picture about to happen because if it's happening at the moment, you first observe the scene. Maybe you'll get the picture. But usually, you can't.

JB: You wrote in *Ordinary Miracles* that a good photographer really needs only one camera and one lens. Yet, when we passed your darkroom, I noticed a 4 x 5 enlarger and 35mm enlarger, and in the course of our conversation, you've mentioned both large and small-format cameras.

LS: I really shot off my mouth about simplicity in that essay. What I was really trying to say is that you don't need a lot of fancy equipment. When I went to New York as a boy and began doing serious photography, I had one camera and one lens, and I did an extensive body of work. In our consumer society, there's a tendency for young photographers to think that equipment is going to do it all. They tell themselves, "I can't really do good work unless I have this camera or that lens." And it's not true. Young photographers really need only one camera and one lens.

But lately, I've come to understand that you can't be a conscious primitive. I'm sophisticated enough in terms of my technical knowledge to know that certain kinds of images require certain kinds of tools. This is the first real darkroom I've ever had. I've always worked in kitchens and closets and bathrooms, on top of the sink. And I now have four cameras and six lenses. I'm finally nicely equipped.

So I guess I was a little deceptive in writing that passage. But as advice to young photographers, I think it's valid.

JB: How did you discover photography?

LS: When I was a little kid, my mother had a tiny vest-pocket Kodak. I took family snapshots and so on with it but never thought too much about it. Then, when I was ten, a friend came over with a twin lens reflex. I pointed the camera at some trees and looked down into it. What immediately struck me was that for some strange reason the trees I saw through the camera were infinitely more interesting than the trees I saw when I looked up. I didn't understand why, but I was hooked. I had to have a twin lens reflex.

JB: How did you get involved in filmmaking?

LS: It just seemed a logical next step after working as a writer and a still photographer. I started out as a poet. Then I got hooked on photography. I put together that first book, went to New York, freelanced, and starved. I was constantly hocking my camera. I'd type a story on my typewriter, and then I'd hock the typewriter to redeem the camera. Then, just before the war, I got a job in Puerto Rico, with a real, regular wage, working for the National Youth Administration. I was a photographer and edited the agency journal. Part of my assignment was to make a 16mm film on the work of the agency with young people and venereal disease. Then I went into the army. I didn't have an opportunity to make films while I was in the army, but I did a lot of still photography and freelance writing. After the war, I went to USC [University of Southern California] on the GI bill and studied film.

JB: Why did you choose to get into filmmaking, rather than continue working in still photography?

LS: Partly it was the money, partly the glamour, and naturally, if you're a photographer, you want to make films. You reach a larger audience.

I never finished my Master's thesis at USC because I was offered a chance to photograph my first 35mm film. I did that, then worked in films and in some television for the next twelve years. Then, UCLA invited me to teach film and photography as it relates to film. I've been doing that for fourteen years. Now, my heart is pretty much back with still photography and photographic books. I intend to produce a book or an exhibition a year for the rest of my life. I've got a backlog of six large projects in the works.

JB: Have you always been so prolific?

LS: Well, I've always been productive, but during the past three years, I've really experienced an explosion of energy.

JB: You've successfully integrated still photography and motion pictures, as well as integrated still photography and writing.

LS: Yes, if there's some particular value to the work I've done in film, it's that I first used still photographs in motion pictures. Actually, people had used them before, as inserts to give information, but I was the first to use photographs as a director uses a live action scene, with the camera moving into the photograph, cutting to the next, moving across images, and so on. *The True Story of the Civil War* was made entirely from civil war photographer Matthew Brady's photographs, as well as those of a few other photographers. I thought this was a most valid way of telling history because instead of dressing people up in costumes and building studio sets, we could really see the actual historical event as it happened one hundred years ago through the eyes of people who were actually there. The film won me my first Academy Award and a little money, but not much. I've never made much money with film.

JB: Didn't you further develop storytelling through still photographs in *The Black Fox,* a film about the rise and fall of Hitler's Third Reich, for which you won another Academy Award?

LS: Yes, and in *The Naked Eye,* a documentary about photography, and particularly about Edward Weston.

JB: It sounds as if you've come full circle from still photography to filmmaking, then back to still photography. Why did you stop making films?

LS: Well, eventually I had my own production company with a full-time staff of five. I was very busy, but I didn't feel creative. I found I was spending 95 percent of my time on contracts, lawyers, casting, distribution, and so on, and I didn't like it. Only 5 percent of my time was going into creative work. At the same time, I was doing still photography and getting more and more excited about it. So I decided to get out of there. Maybe it was sour grapes, and if someone gave me $10 million to make a movie, I'd consider it, but I don't think so. To make a film takes a year out of your life—most of it spent on peripheral chores.

JB: Are there any photographers who you feel have been particular influences on your work?

LS: Paul Strand, Edward Weston, Walker Evans, who was a very great street photographer, Alfred Stieglitz, whom I was fortunate enough to meet shortly before he died. I met Edward Weston in 1946 or 1947. I was much closer to Weston than I was to Stieglitz, whom I met just the one time. I spent many days with Weston. As I said, he was the subject of *The Naked Eye,* but I went to him years before I made the film. I also met Ansel Adams at about the same time and have learned from him ever since.

JB: Have you always sought out photographers you've admired?

LS: Yes, I have.

JB: Why?

LS: Well, I guess I first saw their work and then felt it was very important to get a sense of what kind of person would do that kind of work. But I'll tell you something about this business of admiring other artists. Young writers, photographers, and painters often look at another artist's work and tell themselves, "I could *never* do something like that. It's beyond my capabilities." Well, the truth is, it isn't. We've all got more talent than we can possibly use. I don't feel awed by the work of any other contemporary photographer. I *did* when I was younger. I just told myself I'd do my best, learn from other artists, imitate them, get their vibes, but eventually you go with your own muse.

JB: Do you think you find your own muse by going through the process of imitating?

LS: I think it's a necessary part of the process. An infant learns by imitating the mother and father. A young artist learns by imitating a master. If you're a writer, your writing is certainly shaped by what you've read, and then, as you progress, you move on into your own style. I first imitated Stieglitz.

JB: Consciously or subconsciously?

LS: Well, maybe neither. I was simply aware of his work while I was working. With Weston, I never worked like him. He used an 8 x 10 camera with a tripod, and his vision was very different from mine. The principal thing I learned from him was how a photographic artist can live and work, what qualities of dedication or simplicity or passion or range of view are possible. I guess we all have role models, and Edward Weston was one of mine. Another thing I learned from him is that really good artists and photographers, if they feel truly secure about their own work, can look at someone else's work that's very different from their own and understand that this is another way to use the medium. Weston was able to do that with me. I showed him my work, and he gave me very valuable criticism. His door was always open, and I valued that.

JB: One last question, and then we'll let you get back to your many projects. Why do you photograph in black-and-white rather than color?

LS: There are several factors that keep my away from color. Its archivalness is questionable, for one thing. Everybody's home snapshots from ten years ago are now faded and ugly, and I don't want to make pictures that aren't going to live physically. Also, color is a literal medium. It has to correspond fairly closely to reality—although certain photographers have exaggerated it to good effect—and what I've been trying to do, in terms of form and making a photograph *really* happen, has to do with a certain amount of abstraction or transcendence from the material. In black-and-white, it seems to work better. I can print dark. I can print light. I can work for contrast—all on the same kind of subject matter. And I've still got so much to learn about black-and-white. I'm learning all the time.

What it boils down to is this: With the exception of a certain small body of work by a certain few photographers, it seems to me that color photography is always prose and that black-and-white photography has at least the possibility of becoming poetry.

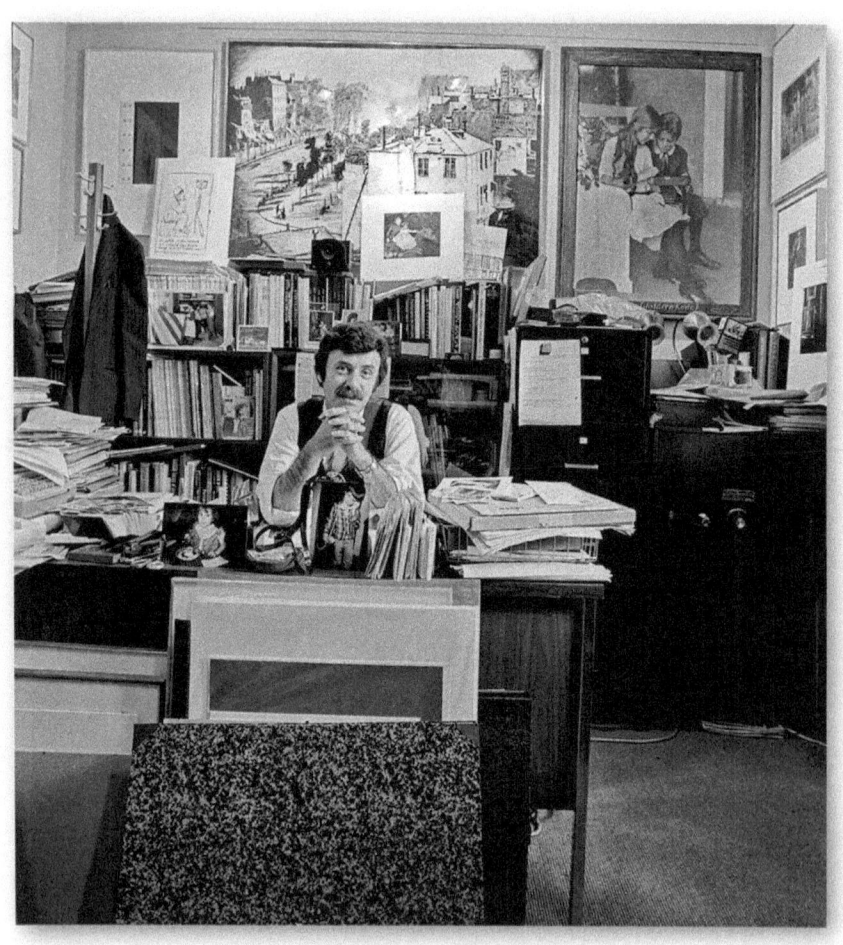

Photo by Kurt Fishback

LEE D. WITKIN (1935–1984)

A Candid Chat

Published May/June 1982

In 1969, Lee D. Witkin quit his comfortable job as a writer for a construction magazine. Against all advice, and with only a few thousand dollars and the then not widely accepted conviction that photography is art, he opened the Witkin Gallery. To everyone's surprise, even Witkin's, the gallery prospered. It's now New York City's oldest photography gallery and has established residence at a prestigious address in midtown Manhattan after outgrowing humbler settings twice. Now, a successful gallery and two books (*The Photography Collector's Guide* and *A Ten Year Salute*) behind him, Witkin grumbles about overhead and overtime, seethes about unscrupulous dealers, would-be artists, and status-seekers, and generally regrets the passing of the old days. But through it all, his pioneering spirit still glimmers as he contemplates the next step in his gallery's evolution.

JB: Would you say you represent photographs or photographers?

LW: I represent photographers, and actually, that's changing now so that I'm representing creative people, period. What's happened is that we've gone from one extreme to another. In 1969, hardly anyone paid any attention to the great photographers in America and Europe, and they were delighted when I called them. I had a little hole-in-the-wall gallery and no background as a dealer, yet I was able to get photographs by Steichen, Ansel Adams, the Westons, Imogen Cunningham, Lartigue, Bill Brandt, Brassai, and many other major photographers. There wasn't any door that was really closed, and the humility on the part of these great photographers was truly astounding. Imogen Cunningham was asking fifteen dollars for her prints and was pleased to get that much. Now it's a different story. I think it must be emphasized that photography is just a medium and merely because one takes pictures and calls oneself a photographer doesn't mean one has the right to call oneself an artist deserving of shows and books. So, if I emphasize the individual and move the medium to the second line, maybe some of the current crop of young people will realize it's the artist who counts, not the medium.

JB: Let's get back to 1969. In *A Ten Year Salute,* a number of people who've been involved with the Witkin Gallery since it opened reminisce about those first ten years, and many of those who were around during the planning stages remember being dubious that the gallery would succeed. With all that negative reinforcement, what made you so sure?

LW: What was important to me was never the gallery's success. In fact, I didn't expect it to succeed. I was doing it because I wanted to have made an effort, sometime in my life, to get involved in something I originated and cared about, rather than going from college to a job and finding myself sixty years old and my life over. I didn't care whether it worked out or not, as long as I'd made the attempt.

JB: How old were you then?

LW: I was very old. That's one of the reasons I started the gallery when I did. I was thirty-three.

JB: *Very old?*

LW: When you're a teenager and then all of a sudden you're thirty-three, it's frightening. I felt that if I didn't change my life in my early thirties, there was no hope of ever changing my life.

JB: What were you doing up to your thirty-third birthday?

LW: I graduated from New York University as an English major and took a job near home in South Orange, New Jersey, as a news editor for *Constructioneer* magazine. It was a good job, and it was really interesting. I drove around the Mid-Atlantic States covering construction projects. I was paid well and had all kinds of benefits—Blue Cross, profit sharing, retirement, and a car allowance. There were other reasons for taking and keeping the job. We had a hardship at home, and I had to be around most of the time. Then, when my parents died, I was free for the first time in my life. During the two years after my mother died, I saved all the money I could, and then opened the Witkin Gallery.

JB: Your first show was a group show, and you exhibited the work of Scott Hyde, George Krause, Duane Michals, George Tice, and Burk Uzzle. Was there any particular reason for choosing these photographers to mark the gallery's debut?

LW: It happened basically by chance. I saw Burk Uzzle's work in a magazine. I met George Tice by chance. Then, when the gallery was actually open, people would come in and ask me to get the work of this or that photographer. Soon, the customer's requests led me to approach the photographers they were interested in. During the gallery's first summer, I closed up for July and went to California, where I met Cole Weston, Imogen Cunningham, Judy Dater, Jack Welpott, and a lot of other fine photographers. That resulted in my representing them.

So, for a long time, it was chance that determined who we represented. Then, somewhere in the middle, it became obvious that we had to be a little more selective, only because you can't handle everyone in the world. You take stock of what you have and fill in areas you're weak in. If you have a couple of photographers who represent one kind of work, you say no if someone working in the same way comes along.

JB: In glancing over the list of photographers who've exhibited at Witkin, I noticed that as time progressed, you held fewer and fewer group shows and more and more one- or two-photographer shows. Any particular reason for that?

LW: Well, in the beginning the individual photographer wasn't that much of a draw. Then too, a lot of photographers, young as well as old, were in possession of very few of their prints. I'd get just a handful of prints from them. Later on, when it became obvious things were taking off, photographers wanted larger representations of their work and were able to provide more prints. They also began to decide they wanted to show alone, rather than with other people.

JB: When did you first realize that the gallery was a success?

LW: Actually, not until 1974 or 1975. I kept working so hard, and things kept going so fast, it never occurred to me that it was going to last. I suppose I never let myself believe it before then because I'm very cautious. I don't trust good fortune. But by then, I had to believe it. I don't know if I could say I was delighted. Doing something that you don't have the responsibility of believing in is like living a fantasy, but when you know it's real, that it's going to last, at least for a while, the fantasy flees, and you find yourself saying, "Well, this is success, and now I've got to pay my dues."

JB: Is that what you're doing now? Paying your dues?

LW: Absolutely. I'm working harder than I've ever worked. I have more overhead. And a lot of the joy is gone. It's the nature of man to grow disillusioned with his routines and the things he has. I still love what I'm doing. I really do, but every once in a while, I get the feeling that I've had enough. But then I ask myself, what would I rather do?

JB: When did other photography galleries begin to follow you?

LW: Marge Neikrug opened her gallery a year or so after me, and Light Gallery opened about two and a half years after I did. Some of the major art galleries decided to show one or two photographers, as well as artists working in other mediums. Then the whole thing really exploded. There were galleries opening everyplace. We'd get four, five phone calls a day in the midseventies: "Hi, I'm calling from Timbuktu, and I'm opening a photography gallery. Will you tell me how to do it?"

It was amazing. People thought we were in the business of advising. And we got hurt because we *did* help a lot of people. We lent a lot of work that we either didn't get back and never got paid for, or got back in shabby condition. This has hurt me very much, and I've learned that I can't give prints to people, even friends, because the gallery can't afford to lose that kind of money. This causes resentment. For some reason, people feel that because I was the first and I'm succeeding, I have a moral obligation to help them. You'd be surprised what people decide you owe them.

JB: What struck me when I first walked in here was how different the Witkin Gallery looks from any other photography gallery I've visited. It's comfortable, with couches in the center of the room and bookcases full of books, as well as photographs. Nowadays, it seems the fashion in gallery décor is toward the cold and stark, with white walls and empty floor space. You were the first photography gallery to really become a success. Why do you think more galleries haven't copied your "look"?

LW: Well, you build a certain kind of nest if you're a certain kind of bird. I like comfort, and I like clutter. I collected etchings and paintings and books and things for about ten years before I opened the gallery. The galleries and bookstores I visited where I was comfortable and people were pleasant brought me a great deal of joy. The places where the noses were up in the air and there was a kind of sterility— I went in and I left quickly. So when I started my gallery, I wanted to incorporate the things that made me happy in other galleries. It's my nature to want to talk to people and sit down with them. A lot of people feel there's a lack of dignity in that. They feel that if you're not cold and arrogant, you're not as dignified as you should be. It's ridiculous. Who are you going to impress with white walls? I hate to go into a gallery where no one even looks up when you come in to acknowledge your presence, to acknowledge you're human. And art is the most human of all things in the world. A lot of very stupid, ignorant people are involved in the art world. They don't know what they're dealing with, and their way of handling questions is to be arrogant, so they're not exposed. I just never bought that.

JB: Do you frequent any of the other photography galleries?

LW: I used to. There used to be a small golden group. Everyone came to my openings, and I went to everybody else's. That's when there were three or four galleries in town. But as happens when success raises its head, you begin to have fallings out. It got to be so that if I went to other galleries, I would be insulted, or my brain would be picked, or I'd be fawned over. It made me uncomfortable, and I didn't see why I should go and experience that. Life's too short. I do go to other galleries, but they aren't in my field, and I maintain friendships with other dealers all over the country. The galleries here in New York just became too competitive. A lot of things happened that I couldn't forgive. Photographers were asked to leave me to go to these other galleries. My nature is such that when that happens, fine, but I can't be a friend with someone who, behind my back, is trying to take my photographers away from me. So it was easier not to see these people than to see them under hypocritical circumstances.

JB: In terms of fame and power, do you think newer galleries have eclipsed the Witkin Gallery?

LW: I've always been panicky about something like that happening, but it was inevitable. I've never had a lot of money, and money means power. It means being able to go to an artist and say, "I'll give you so much more money." Since most artists need money, they'll go. I've never had a vast amount of money or some kind of syndicate behind me, and some galleries are very, very rich and do incredible things. They produce fantastic catalogs, mount fabulous shows and advertise, send shows abroad, offer artists a guaranteed income. I've had to accept that. I'm not in that league. First of all, don't forget, I opened my gallery in a hole in the wall with six thousand dollars. So the fact that I've come this far is a miracle. I've never had any pretensions about being a giant because I just didn't have that kind of money. Now I realize I wouldn't want to be a giant. It's not in my nature to wield that kind of power. No, I don't feel I've been eclipsed, because I've been singular and different. I stand for the quiet qualities that these other galleries don't have—which some people still admire— and that's my uniqueness.

JB: Let's talk a bit about your *modus operandi*. What are your criteria for representing a photographer?

LW: Well, as I said before, a lot of the relationships evolved by chance, but basically, I have to respond to the work. It's really a gut feeling. I work closely with my staff, and there have been cases where I did not personally respond to the work. I had to be a little more objective and say even so, I believe this is good and important. It doesn't "hit" me, but I have to step outside myself. Lee Friedlander, for example. I never truly responded to his work, but we did represent him for a while because I felt it was my limitation rather than his. Only time will tell.

I don't do that very often. I like to exhibit what I like, and because my taste is eclectic, I feel I can do that and still have a broad range. I like old-fashioned work, historical work, mixed media, color, black-and-white. We represent all kinds of styles and all kinds of photographers— young, old, middle aged, famous, not so famous, European, American.

JB: Do you have a personal favorite photograph or photographer?

LW: There are lots of photographers I particularly respond to. When I was a child I often came into the city with my mother, so Berenice Abbott's New York is very, very meaningful to me, and there are a lot of her pictures in my house. I also have a lot of Imogen Cunningham's and George Tice's work. But I have thousands of prints in my collection that I just bought because I liked them, so it's very difficult to pinpoint favorites. I have a lot of favorites. Probably more favorites than anybody else.

JB: Do your feelings toward photographs change over time?

LW: Usually not. My nature isn't such that I suddenly turn and say, "I don't like this anymore, and I don't know why I ever liked it." I'm very sentimental. If I like something, I usually go on liking it forever. That's why my place is such a mess.

JB: When you look at a photographer's work, is your response to it colored by whether or not you feel it will be saleable?

LW: No, and it never has been because I don't know what's saleable. Barbara Morgan was in my second show, and I remember that as we were looking at her prints, she would pick one out and say, "I'm sure *this* will sell." In most cases, something else sold. Now when people say, "This will sell," I smile. It's a statement you can't make. I'm constantly astounded by what does and does not sell. And it isn't really important. If we put up a good show with a lot of images, hopefully enough people will come in, and each will respond to something different, and we'll sell enough. But what's happened, in fact, is that collectors all want the same picture now. They're not interested in buying a good image that hasn't been reproduced to death or isn't in a museum. They want famous pictures. So not only can I not predict what will sell but also when an image becomes popular and everybody wants it, it's very depressing. I get people who know nothing about the medium and who weren't inclined to collect art to begin with but want what they see in their friends' houses. They're keeping up with the Joneses. Art deserves more than that. For the first five to seven years, we did get people who were interested in photography for the right reasons. They didn't have to be convinced it was an art, and there was no prestige in collecting it because photography was still considered a stepchild. But now that photography's fashionable, you get people who know nothing and want to buy it for the wrong reasons. Sadly, the people who used to buy for the right reasons have been priced out of the market.

JB: What images are most popular?

LW: Jerry Uelsmann's "Cloud Room," Judy Dater's "Imogen and Twinka," George Tice's "Petit Mobil Stations and Water Tower," Ansel's "Moonrise," Edward Weston's "Pepper 30." I could go on and on. Each photographer has one or two classics that people want.

JB: And the more popular it is the more expensive it is.

LW: Yes. In a lot of cases the photographers up the price of particular images hoping to limit sales. Ironically enough, this doesn't stop people from buying. A lot of people want them even more. It's very peculiar. Within a certain context, price has very little relationship to salability.

JB: Do you set a limit on the number of prints a photographer can make from any given negative?

LW: No, never. Photography is a graphic multiple medium and the negative quality does not diminish on subsequent printings as the plate for an etching might. And over the years, papers change, photographers' interpretations of their negatives change. I know most of the people I represent, and I know they don't print indiscriminately. Most photographers, if they're concerned with their work, aren't about to sabotage its value by overprinting. Also, it's very hard to make a print. People say, "Well, you can make thousands and thousands." Yes, theoretically it *is* possible, but a photographer would go out of his mind spending all that time in the darkroom printing the same image over and over. Actually, my biggest problem is getting the photographer to make one print, not that he may make too many.

JB: I understand you've made it a policy not to review the work of photographers who drop in unannounced, portfolios in hand.

LW: What we require before we look at a portfolio is a letter of recommendation from someone in the field to show us that someone who knows what he's talking about thinks highly of this person's work. Then we make an appointment at our mutual convenience to look at the work. A lot of people are incredibly selfish. They walk in the door with their portfolios and demand immediate attention. When they don't get it, they're furious. That's too bad. It seems to me that our conditions are reasonable.

We do take new work occasionally, but less increasingly, because we just don't have enough space, and the work that's being produced today by most people is very derivative. It's very difficult to find a bright new eye. I recently judged several shows around the country, and I could tell who most applicants had studied with, or what work had impressed them. Which isn't necessarily bad. It just never occurred before because there wasn't the vast communication there is today with books, workshops, exhibitions, etc. When I started out, I had virtually the pick of 130 years of work. The photographers we represented the first few years had been working for decades and had bodies of work. All the others had dropped away, so it was obvious whose work was important. Now it's a completely different scene. Instead of looking for one needle in a little tiny pile of hay, you're looking for one needle in a field of haystacks.

JB: Is that an additional frustration?

LW: I'm not frustrated by it. It's the natural course of things. In the old days, it was very easy to recognize the great photographers—Brassai, Lartigue, Bill Brandt, Ansel, Imogen, and Ralph Steiner—and love their work and want to show them. It's not so easy to look at the portfolio of a twenty-three-year-old who's done interesting and promising work, but nothing really important, and know he may yet become a great photographer. And if you don't tell these young people that they're great and you'd like to show them, they get very upset.

Another important thing: talent is a gift, a rare gift. No matter how good a person you are, or how hard you work, if you don't have it you don't have it. Most young people today are sadly unaware of art history and of other art forms that are now being practiced. The older photographers were very much aware of art history. They had dialogues with writers, musicians, and painters. Edward Weston came to life when he met, through Margrethe Mather, the poets and actors out on the West Coast. Manuel Alvarez Bravo in his eighties is constantly interested in seeing other artists' work. His ego is satisfied. He's sure enough of himself to be able to respond to what someone else is doing. A lot of young people aren't. You look at their work, and you start talking about someone else, and they immediately tune out. It's too bad, because it means their own work is going to suffer from a certain amount of sterility that's inevitable unless you're aware of a broad number of things. You really cannot be a major artist unless you're aware of life around you.

JB: Over the past twelve years, you've gotten to know a number of this century's greatest photographers on a personal basis, and I imagine you've got some very interesting stories to tell about them. Any plans for immortalizing them in book form in the future?

LW: I did a little bit of that in *A Ten Year Salute,* but maybe in ten or twenty years when a lot of people are dead, I'll be freer to be more candid. I don't promise an exposé, but it should make for interesting, lively reading. I look forward to writing something like that, and I'll be able to get a little bit of revenge. I think some people who shall remain nameless here have behaved very badly, and I would like to make that public. But really, most people have been wonderful. It'll be a more sweet than bitter memoir.

JB: What do you envision for the Witkin Gallery's future?

LW: I'd like to diversify and show nonphotographic prints. I'm very into graphics of the twenties, thirties, and forties, which, by the way, are importantly related to the FSA photographs and Berenice Abbott's work. I think people should be aware that photographers weren't working in isolation…that they were working with the same style and subject matter as a lot of painters and printmakers. Now, after twelve years of saying that photography is art, I think there should be a shift into relating it to its time and other arts, and I'd like to be involved with that. So right now, my main concern is to integrate prints other than photographs into the gallery and hopefully, in the process, get a new and different audience that would never come to the gallery to see just photographs. And hopefully, people who come to see the photographs won't be horrified to see something nonphotographic and may actually begin to relate photographs to nonphotographic work. That's what I see happening in the next few years.

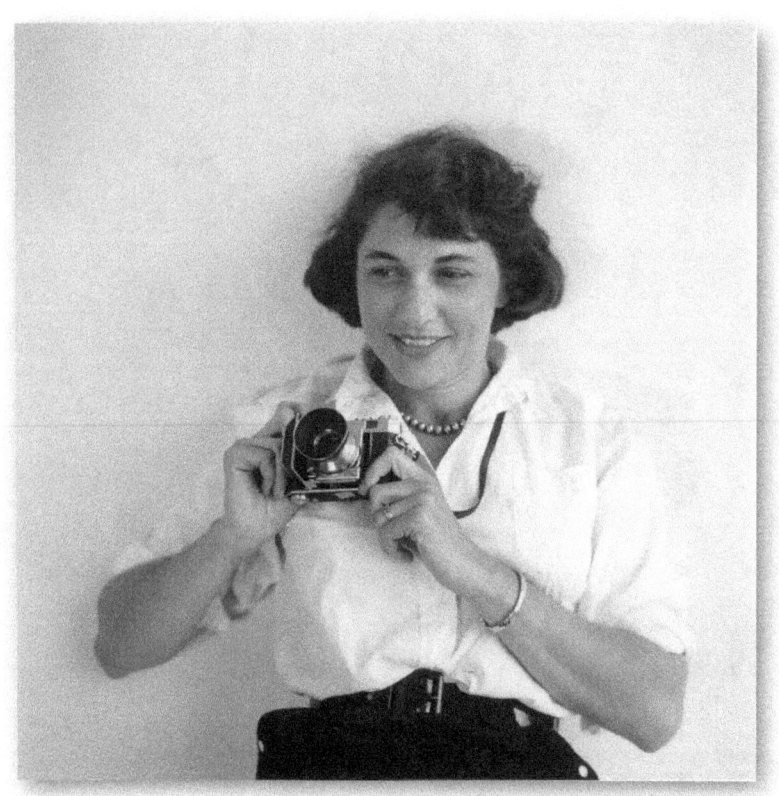

Photo by Morris Engel

RUTH ORKIN (1921–1985)

Candor and Candids

Published September/October 1982

Ruth Orkin will tell you that a successful photojournalist is alternately a photographer and a salesperson. Self-taught in both occupations, Orkin's methods haven't always been textbook. Even so, shortly after she decided to become a photojournalist in the midforties, her candid photographs of musicians, celebrities, and ordinary people were appearing in all the major picture magazines and in many of Steichen's Museum of Modern Art exhibitions, including "The Family of Man."

But photography wasn't Orkin's first career choice. A child of Hollywood, she'd always wanted to be a filmmaker, and when she was honored as one of the Top Ten Women Photographers in the United States in 1959, she'd already thrown over photojournalism for her first love. In 1953, she cowrote and codirected the award-winning *Little Fugitive*. Then she retired to raise a family, although the recent publication of *A World Through My Window* and *A Photo Journal* shows her camera has never been far away.

Now, Orkin is devoting her full attention to photography again, and in addition to teaching and exhibiting, she has eight more book projects in various stages of completion. In her Manhattan apartment high above Central Park, she talked, with characteristic candor, about her life and times.

JB: Since you're the daughter of a silent-film actress, and you grew up near Hollywood, wasn't it almost inevitable that the local preoccupation—movies—would affect your choice of career?

RO: Yes, I always wanted to make films. But I discovered you had to be a member of the Cinematographer's Union to run a camera, and the union didn't allow women members.

JB: Do you think you would have become a still photographer anyway if you'd been allowed in the union?

RO: No. I'm sure my whole life would have been different. Recently, my editor at Viking pointed out something I never consciously realized. She said that I have more photo sequences than any other photographer she knows. She attributed this to my interest in the movies. After I made *Little Fugitive* with my husband, Morris Engel, in 1953, I almost lost interest in still photography completely.

JB: Why was that?

RO: You've got plenty of power with still photographs, especially if you get published in the magazines with circulations in the millions. But with a movie, you can actually hear your power in the audience's reaction. You know, I used to debate with myself when I had a photograph I knew would sell. I'd say to myself, "*This Week* has a circulation of twelve million and pays $300 a page. *Life* has a circulation of nine million and pays $150 a page. Should I sell it to *Life* for prestige or *This Week* for coverage?" It depended on what I was selling. If I were trying to sell images of Israel, for example, I'd give them to *This Week*. It was often very hard to make a choice, especially if I needed the money.

JB: Even though you say you wouldn't have become a photographer if the Cinematographer's Union had been open to you, you seem to have always been fascinated with photography. You were taking photographs when you were ten and developing them at twelve.

RO: I not only developed them, but later on I mixed chemicals from scratch. I didn't have any money—we were on relief—so I did it at high school where they had all the chemicals.

JB: How did you learn technique? Did you emulate established photographers?

RO: Well, I couldn't really, because most people were using Rolleis, and the Rollei viewfinder drove me crazy. But when I was eighteen and still in Los Angeles, I spent a lot of time looking through camera annuals in the Los Angeles Library. The Leica annuals, as opposed to the *U.S. Camera* annuals, had more of the kinds of pictures I liked because they were all 35mm. I could see that you could do things with a 35mm camera that you couldn't with other cameras. Those were the pictures I wanted to take—pictures that were natural, candid, real, human, humorous—where people weren't aware of the camera. That's when I first saw my husband's pictures—in *U.S. Camera*. He was able, for some unknown reason, to do the same thing with a Rollei. I remembered his name. In fact, I memorized it. On the streetcar coming home, I kept saying "Morris Engel" because it was a lot easier than "Alfred Eisenstaedt." Now isn't that prophetic?

JB: Did you ever take any photography classes?

RO: Every time I tried to take a course, I'd leave after about three classes. It just wasn't relevant. Nobody taught photojournalism in those days, and I knew my future was with a 35mm camera. I was just waiting until I could get one.

JB: So basically, you taught yourself by trial and error?

RO: Yes. I remember the first time Morris came into my darkroom— which was really my bathroom—my reels were just sitting in the developer. I used to leave them in there a long time. He said, "What are you doing? You're not supposed to leave the reels in the developer overnight!" And that's how I learned—a little bit here, a little bit there. I also used to learn just by talking to men in photo stores, because if you were a serious photographer, and you were female and attractive, you could get all kinds of free advice. There weren't many female photographers in those days. When I joined the ASMP [American Society of Magazine Photographers] in 1947, there were thirty women out of three hundred members.

JB: How did you get started as a professional photographer?

RO: Well, I worked for a while as a nightclub photographer. Then I went from door to door, photographing babies. On my own, I went up to the Tanglewood Music Festival in 1946 to photograph the musicians. I wrote ahead to tell them I was coming and got a letter back telling me not to bother. I went anyway. I took my cello and pretended I was a music student. I made enough money with my Tanglewood photographs to buy a 35mm camera.

JB: Up to that time, did you ever doubt your choice of a career?

RO: There's a natural kind of arrogance that goes with being twenty-two. During that time, I worked as an assistant for someone who was photographing Lenny Bernstein, and I said to myself, "Someday he's going to be posing for me!" I was so sure of myself, so cocky. My friends were always telling me to shut up, or think before I spoke. But you've got to be able to convince people you're better than someone else if you want to succeed. You've got to have a lot of ego. Every artist does. Back then, though, I didn't think of it as ego. I knew I saw certain things, and I wanted to take pictures of them, and I just wanted everybody else to see what I saw. I would get very enthusiastic about certain subjects, and I'd be selling what interested me. Once, up at *Look*, I said to my editor, "Do you know who the greatest, the most important chorale conductor in the world is? It's Bob Shaw, and here are the pictures." He ran them. The most important thing is the picture, of course. They have to be able to sell themselves. But I know my enthusiasm for the photos helped sell them. I never had an agent.

JB: Did you always pick a subject that interested you, photograph it, and then sell the photographs?

RO: Half and half. I did work on assignment. I photographed a lot of "How America Lives" stories for *Ladies Home Journal*. They'd send me to live with and photograph a typical American family for two weeks. The writer usually went beforehand, so there wouldn't be too many strangers around. Then I'd go and just shoot pictures.

But other times, I'd go looking for possibilities. I'll tell you how it worked. When I went to Israel on the first El Al press junket, for example, I decided to do a story on one of their pilots. I had fifteen pilots to pick from, but only three of them were Jewish, and naturally El Al wanted me to do a Jewish pilot. I was sitting in the Lydda airport, and I saw this guy—a pilot—walk in who was a mixture of Burt Lancaster and Kirk Douglas. He was so relaxed and so attractive. To be relaxed is one of the most important requirements of a really great subject. I said to myself, "Please, God, let him be Jewish." And he was!

One of the reasons I decided to do that story was because food supplies in Israel then were very limited—we only had four or five staples to choose from every day—and I knew pilots had great food in their refrigerators. So I got a great photo story at the same time that I got to eat strawberries from Africa and all kinds of other delicacies. The story ran five pages in *Cosmopolitan*.

JB: Your photograph of Einstein is one of your most popular. Was that on assignment?

RO: Yes, that was lovely. I was hired to photograph him at a luncheon, shaking hands with each of one hundred men who had donated money to Albert Einstein University. I sat and had lunch with him. Meanwhile, outside there was a big press conference, and all the male news photographers wanted to know why I was inside at the luncheon, and they weren't. One of the main reasons I got the job was because just about everyone worked with flash then, and they wanted someone who could work without flash. To get enough light, I got the kitchen staff to get up on ladders and put aluminum foil all over the ceiling. It was a tremendous job because the ceiling was arched. Then I bounced my floodlight off the foil. I just barely made it. I took the pictures with Plus-X at f/2 and 1/60.

JB: One of the hallmarks of an Orkin photograph is the candidness of the subject. I was therefore very surprised to learn that many of your photographs are actually staged—for example, "American Girl in Italy." *Publisher's Weekly* described it as "a candid, incisive, storytelling photo that, in its genre, has never been topped." Isn't there something a little bit…devious…about staging photojournalism to appear candid?

RO: I don't like that word. The ultimate result is what counts, and if it's a statement that's honest and true, what the heck difference does it make? What's devious about that? I never said that shot was candid. The girl in the photo and I were running around looking for pictures to depict the frustrations of traveling alone, as opposed to what the glamorous travel posters and brochures were saying it was supposedly like. We came across all those fellows spread out like that. I didn't put them there. All I did was tell the guy on the motorcycle, who spoke English, to tell the others not to look at the camera. I only made two exposures because, if you'll notice, I'm in the middle of the intersection, and I didn't want to get hit.

JB: What are the most important elements of a good photograph?

RO: Number one, it should stop you. Number two, it should be interesting. I see too many photographs these days that just aren't interesting. There's nothing happening. There's a bench, or a piece of cloud, or litter someplace. Who needs that in this day and age? To me, the important thing isn't that a photograph should be simply beautiful. Photographs should have messages. Artists shouldn't spend their time making pictures out of nonsense when we've got this nuclear thing hanging over our heads.

I think Paul Schutzer did the best photo story I've ever seen. It was on Vietnam, and *Life* printed it in 1966. He photographed under fire, yet every picture could have been hung on a gallery wall. My son was six years old when he saw the photographs. There was one where a group of women were cowering because bombs were falling. He said, "Why don't they take the women and children out of Vietnam? If the men want to fight, why are the women and children around?" Isn't that sensible?

JB: You write in *A Photo Journal* that because you're a woman, you've been able to get responses from your male subjects that a male photographer wouldn't have gotten. In that sense, being a woman was an asset, but did it ever hold you back in any way?

RO: It sure did! I remember being sent out to shoot Dmitri Shosta-kovich when he first came here after the war. There was a big press conference, and I was the only woman there. I'll tell you, a woman is no match for strong men fighting to get a position to photograph someone. I'm all for the Equal Rights Amendment, but don't tell me we're equal when it comes to physical strength!

But if you look at my picture of Bob Capa, you can see that in that case it paid to be a woman. When I took that picture, he was flirt-ing with me, so the picture shows off his personality. I think *Fortune* missed the boat years ago when they didn't hire women to shoot men executives and men to shoot women executives.

JB: What do you think about when you're photographing?

RO: I think about whether or not the exposure is right and won-der if somebody is going to move and ruin the whole composition. Afterward, I think about printing, labeling and filing, trying to get published, and money. That's what it's all about. I don't like the idea of people analyzing and reading something into your work. Half the time they're all wet.

JB: Do you do your own printing now?

RO: God forbid. I don't even have the time to get my negatives and pictures filed the way I'd like them. I'm really working hard on that, with the help of an assistant, so I can get my books out. But I've stopped printing. When I tried to do some printing for my first show at Witkin in 1977, I went crazy. It was like a concert pianist who hadn't practiced for twenty years. After two days spent producing unusable prints, I said, this is it. Let somebody else do it.

JB: I see your name in print again and again now, and you're continually referred to as "one of America's most outstanding photographers," or something of the sort. What's your reaction to that?

RO: Ha, ha, ha! Well, I mean it's very nice to be appreciated. Actually, the interesting thing is the meaning these pictures are taking on thirty or forty years after I took them. Of course, a lot of that is because photography has become an art form, so called, and people are paying for it.

JB: I got the impression from *A Photo Journal* that now that you're devoting most of your attention to compiling your photographs in book form, you're for all practical purposes a retired photographer...

RO: Are you kidding? I've never worked so hard at photography in my life! So many people think of photography as just getting behind a camera and pushing a button. When I was working as a photojournalist, I always said that photography was 10 percent taking pictures and 90 percent selling them. Now that there's such a limited market for photojournalism, it's more like 2 percent taking pictures and 98 percent selling them through books and exhibits and so on. Taking the picture is the tip of the iceberg. Making something with the pictures you've taken—like the books I'm working on—is what's really important.

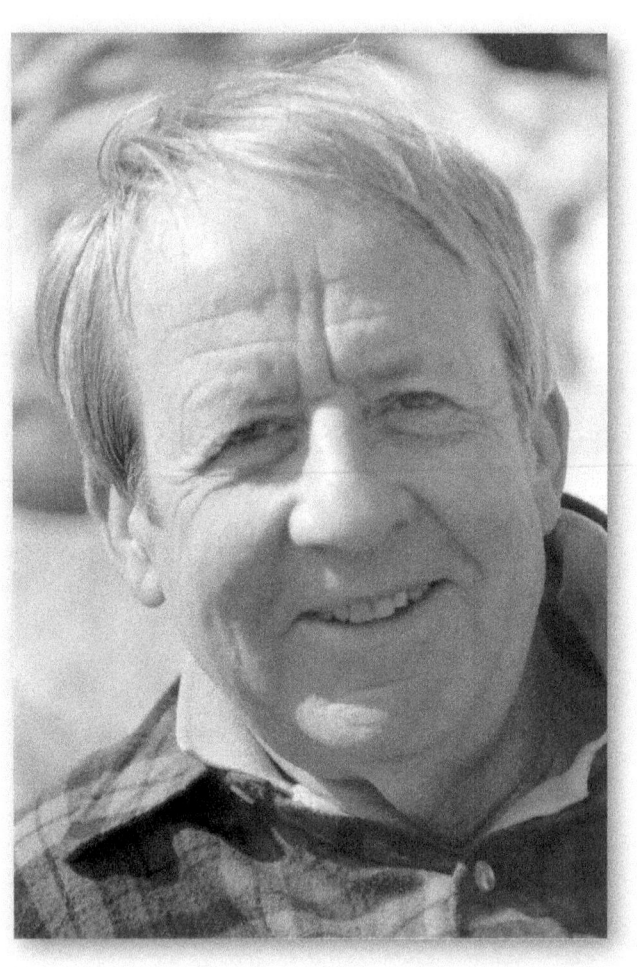

RAY K. METZKER (1931–2014)

A Formalist with Heart

Published December 1982

Black-and-white photographer Ray K. Metzker has spent over twenty years producing a varied body of black-and-white work ranging from single-negative prints to complex composites of up to four hundred images. Though his photographs have found an enthusiastic audience of art critics, curators, and the Guggenheim and NEA [National Endowment for the Arts] committees, they continue to bewilder a larger public. Far from regretting this, Metzker is pleased at having escaped the celebrity he feels has compromised many better-known photographers' work.

JB: Your studies with Aaron Siskind and Harry Callahan at the Institute of Design in Chicago clearly played a major role in your development as an artist. How did you happen to find yourself at the Institute in the first place?

RKM: After I got out of the army, I was intent on continuing my education. I returned to Beloit, where I did my undergraduate work, for a postgraduate semester. But I had done photography in high school and college and just felt so close to it that I thought somewhere, somehow, I should try to expand it. Some people from the Institute came to Beloit to give a lecture. They raved about the program—said that serious, experienced photographers were teaching there, that they were the best, and I wouldn't find anything like it anywhere else. So I went for a visit and met Siskind and Callahan. I was beginning to be open to doing things without knowing the outcome: putting myself in a position where I'd meet people of quality, letting my confidence build step by step until I knew that this was the right challenge, that something was going to happen.

JB: After meeting Siskind and Callahan, you sensed you were putting yourself—

RKM: In very good hands.

JB: The first series of your photographs to attract serious critical attention was your thesis—the Chicago Loop series. How did that project come about?

RKM: All the things I had done up to that time were primarily on assignment in the photojournalistic area. So whether I was working on the high-school newspaper or in the college PR department, people were telling me, "I want you to do this. I want you to do that." It was assignment and business oriented.

JB: And you wanted to put more of your own preoccupations into your photography?

RKM: Yes. That's a change that came about as a result of being at the Institute. When I went there, I continued to think in terms of photojournalism. Then I considered freelancing in the realm of annual reports and working with industry, but still with freedom to make my own decisions.

JB: What made you decide on the Chicago Loop series? I understand it began as a documentary and ended as a statement on photographic form.

RKM: My experience at the school began to open up all these possibilities—working with people and architecture, going in and exploring the unfamiliar. I wanted to do something that had scale to it. It just hit me one day—the idea of this territory that's defined, physically, by the El tracks. Night and day activities. The buildings. Traffic. It's a melting pot. It seemed to be a place where there was everything. It was a question of going in and seeing how I would respond. It's so big that you really can't control it. I don't know that you ever get on top of it really.

JB: You don't feel the series is complete?

RKM: No. In fact, I'm back in Chicago now teaching at Columbia College, and I'm still photographing the Loop. It's never finished. It's just that at some point you're exhausted.

JB: Why did you decide to teach, as opposed to working in commercial photography?

RKM: I knew I wanted to concentrate on ideas of an exploratory nature, rather than service other people's demands.

JB: Does working with students have any effect on your own work?

RKM: It intensifies my resolve.

JB: What do you mean?

RKM: Well, you watch your students responding vaguely, sliding over a point, and you know that you've got to work harder to clarify things to nail them down. Students in general aren't very well focused. I can help them in this area.

JB: You've been credited as a pioneer of a new photographic vocabulary. Was that a conscious goal—using photography in new ways?

RKM: The real goal is the broadening and the deepening. When I apply that to myself, I'm a photographer. And when I'm working, it's important that there's some kind of growth and some kind of broadening of what I can relate to and how I can see things.

JB: You're talking of photography as a personally motivated thing. But a photographer also has an audience to contend with. Do you consider your audience's reaction to your work when you're photographing?

RKM: There's always an audience and an audience always has responses. For myself, I'm always curious how they're going to respond, but there's no way to determine it. I don't work to evoke specific responses.

JB: Your work was once described as "even at its most accessible, difficult to understand."

RKM: Yes, but is the responsibility on the work or on the viewer?

JB: How large is the audience that finds your work accessible?

RKM: Two. My mother and my dog. Seriously, it just isn't a concern. What I believe in is that you follow your own course, based on your interests and beliefs. You don't do this in isolation because you're looking, reading, and hearing. That's the basis of social intercourse. I think it's basic that the individual wants to communicate, but I'm not acting with a special audience in mind. When I act, I'm synthesizing all that I take in with this flexible medium. Something results that you hope engenders discussion and debate. Many exhibitions seem to lose sight of that goal. They get involved in celebrity. They say, "Isn't so and so terrific." It becomes a flexing of muscles, showing off, a display of virtuosity. But it doesn't prompt people to think. I believe the good show is one that stimulates people to think or to debate what's going on. That's difficult for many people because they want to be able to look, identify, categorize, judge, and move on.

JB: So, for viewers to be able to appreciate your photographs, they are going to have to give them some time and thought.

RKM: Yes. I want to build a body of work of which people can say, "Hey, this is something that demands attention. I can't read it according to the last book I read or the last picture I saw. I have to, in a sense, decode it."

JB: Your imagery is so varied, from the Loop series to your Pictus Interruptus series where you held objects in front of the lens to obscure parts of your subject, to the large multi-image composites. Have your concerns changed from series to series? Is each one a new statement and a new challenge to your viewers?

RKM: I think that after a while, when you deal with a body of work, you're going to see some common denominators. The more one works, the more one is aware of the question: Is it really changing? Is each photograph something new, or is it simply another step in the process of clarifying those basic concerns? And it takes a while to understand just what those basic concerns are. I can't state them clearly in words. That's what all the work is about.

At this point photography dealer Laurence G. Miller, who is selling limited editions of Metzker's work and who has been sitting in on the interview, joins in.

LGM: I think that one of the concerns people overlook is your tenderness and concern for humanity. Most people don't see that because of the formalistic nature of your work. People associate coolness with formalism. There's that formalistic resolve to your images, yet your preoccupation with small details reflects caring.

JB: Your photographs also reflect a rather impish sense of humor.

RKM: That's right. They're funny pictures. I may not make such an overt demonstration of it, but I think one of my deepest motivations is a desire to touch, to reach out. That, I think, is the basis for the sensuousness I strive for in a photograph. One wants to *make*—to touch the materials and see them come alive. That certainly belongs to the experience of the artist. You want to know the world you're living in through very specific sensations. That seems to me fundamental to the act of making.

JB: How would you say your photography fits into the photographic "scene" in general? Do you ever feel you and other photographers have polar concerns?

RKM: I would sense that.

JB: Does that matter?

RKM: Every individual yearns for acceptance. That's what communication is all about. But you also want to do what you feel is right. Of course it would be nice if someone else found it of value. I think that's a dilemma for an artist. You want to follow your own course, but you would also like to have it validated.

JB: What happens when it isn't validated? Have there been times when you've felt you were working in a vacuum?

RKM: I found that my multiple images weren't really accepted when they first came out. Certainly not by photographers—they were the last ones to get excited about them. But that's the way the cookie crumbles. I just felt that from what I was seeing in the nonphotographic world, my responses were valid. My world was based on general creative activity—what was going on in music, sculpture, painting, and dance.

JB: Do you think acceptance, both by viewers and your peers, can be debilitating to artistic growth?

RKM: This is the essential paradox of a contemporary artist's life. I think it's true that what's initially sweet often turns out sour, and what's difficult later has its reward. You arrive in terms of success, but then you're stuck. You've lost your options. You have to be more sensitive to your public's expectations. You watch photographers become famous. They build a body of work. They get, say, a two-year PR play—they get a show and maybe the *New York times* will discuss it, the photo magazines will discuss it, they get a Guggenheim and shows around the country. They get a taste of all that, and then it's gone, and the photographer slips into obscurity. It's unfair. It doesn't contribute to serious work.

JB: So photographers really need a sense of their own destiny to keep doing original work these days.

RKM: Yes. I think of "acceptance" as having an audience that wants to share what I've experienced or seen. That calls for looking at work intelligently. Too often, images by well-known photographers are printed and reprinted, and too often the photographer loses interest and the image's original intensity is no longer there. Or papers have changed. Some of the things that belonged to the original image are gone. Say somebody made an 8 x 10 photograph that really took off. Once that has been acknowledged as a super image they, or their dealers, decide to go for an 11 x 14 or a 16 x 20 because it moves the print into a higher price category. But light, focus, and tone are distinct qualities that find a relationship in a given size. The critical collector or curator should also be making those distinctions.

LGM: Ansel Adams's work is a good illustration of this. The prints he was making in the thirties were for the most part no larger than 4 x 5. They are these wonderful small pictures with a very specific idea behind them. Now, in today's marketplace, Ansel is known for his big prints. They really have nothing to do with what he built his reputation on. The small prints are really his genius. The big reprints forty years later are different photographs. Some may argue they're better, some may argue they're worse. With Ray, we're creating limited editions of his prints *now* because if he made them thirty years from now, they'd be different.

RKM: The point is that further down the road I would hope I'd be involved with something more contemporary, and I don't want to interrupt my work and go back. Any given photograph is a telling image because you can see what my concerns were then.

LGM: In an important way, the limited edition philosophy protects the artist. Because if and when you become a celebrity in the market-place, the orders for your work increase significantly, and you're forced to start cranking them out. Not always, but certainly several major photographers have fallen into this trap. By limiting the edition, you provide a safeguard that every print is going to be very high quality. There will never be a compromise because of marketplace demand.

JB: What are you limiting editions to?

RKM: They'll be varied. Some ten, some maybe as high as twenty-five.

LGM: But I think twenty-five will probably be the top limit. Each one will be just right; then Ray will go on to what's next. Also, by limiting editions, it will make the work competitive in an investor's market.

RKM: I don't want this interpreted as just a device to make money. I simply resent the idea that photographers are defined by a few popular images when there are a lot of other images that show concerns that are just as valid. And in current gallery practice, buyers make their decision based on what they see on the gallery wall and how many red dots they see on a print, but that may not be what they get. We want to deal with people who come in, sit down, and spend time with the photographs—who want a comparative experience and come to their conclusions based on firsthand looking. I think this should make col-lecting photographs much more interesting.

LGM: Another thing. Many dealers insist that photography as a busi-ness, in this bear market, must now rely on the corporations. Well, if you go corporate, you're going to forfeit the intimacy of small pho-tographs. I'd rather find clients to appreciate them in their intended scale. To think that bigger is better is to give in to the notion that you can't make something intimate and wonderful and still get people to buy it.

JB: One final question, Ray. You're known for your work in black-and-white, exclusively. Have you experimented with color at all?

RKM: Well, I can't say that I never put a roll of color film in my camera. But I've never really been curious about color simply because I think the black-and-white work medium is unfathomable. I'm skeptical of people who work in more than one medium. I think that in a sense it's showing off: "Look, I can go from one medium to another! I can do cinema! I can do this! I can do that!" It also has a tendency to lead you to the conclusion that you've done everything. Every day, I work in black-and-white, and I know I'll never get to the bottom of it. If I had one hundred years, I don't think I could exhaust the medium.

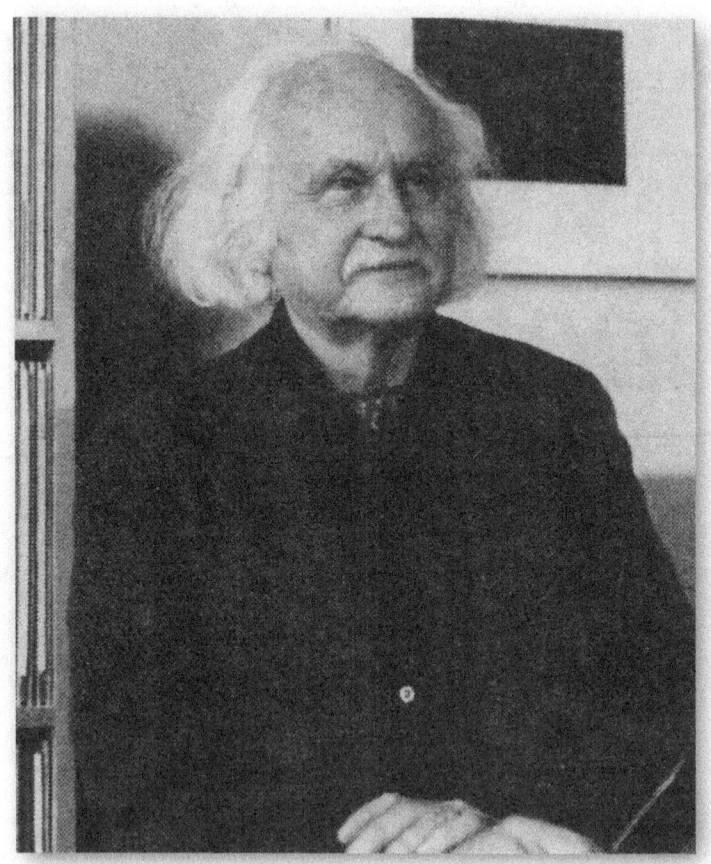

Photo by Janis Bultman

VAL TELBERG (1910–1995)

Unsettling Dreams

Published January/February 1983

Awell-known photography critic once said with academic eloquence and equally academic logic that the medium is by its very nature surreal, and any attempt to manipulate it in the name of surrealism is misguided, redundant. Surreal is an adjective that's often assigned to Val Telberg's photography; it's an adjective, and in fact a social milieu, that he himself is comfortable with, and he does to his images precisely what the abovementioned critic feels is so unnecessary. So to avoid controversy, I've chosen an adjective for Telberg's work that's homely but less likely to distract from the issue at hand: dreamlike. Telberg's photographs are dreamlike.

Even "dreamlike" needs qualification. Telberg's photographs aren't fantasies, like David Hamilton's wet-dream photographs of vague Lolitas, but literally *like dreams,* composed of fragmented images, sometimes recognizable, sometimes not, strung together and, ultimately, not remembered as images but as emotional residues.

And, like dreams, to know them is to abandon oneself to them. They can't be distilled to a message nor can they be absorbed at a glance. As such, they challenge modern viewers, who've been conditioned by the customary arrangement of photographs in books and exhibits to take in a photograph in a moment or two and move on to the next. In the end, Telberg's visual dialog is emotional, not cerebral; subconscious, not conscious.

Telberg came to photography circuitously and, relatively speaking, late. He was born in Russia, bred in China, and immigrated to New York in 1939, working variously as a Chinese antique appraiser and supervisor of a pharmaceutical concern. In his thirties, he went to art school to study painting. To finance his studies, he worked at an amusement park photography concession. "Those were dull days," says Telberg, who, after mastering photography's fundamentals on the job, began entertaining himself by sandwiching negatives.

But he was still at heart a painter and in the forties continued to study art and concentrate on expressing his own version of surrealism's tenets through painting. He used photography primarily as an aid, having found that the days it took to repaint a figure arrangement that wasn't quite right could be eliminated if he used a negative sandwich to blueprint his paintings.

Slowly though, Telberg began to see that as a medium for surreal expression, photography could be an end in itself rather than just a means to an end. In 1950, he knew the final break with painting had come when he moved to France and set up a darkroom instead of an art studio. "A photograph is indisputably a piece of reality," he explains. "A painting may depict reality, but it's not reality. In my photography, where I pervert and corrupt and alter images, it's still, basically, a piece of reality."

Telberg's images are usually montages, composed of bits and pieces of photographs he's taken over the years. He carries with him either his 120-format Bronica or Mamiya and shoots indiscriminately, without plan—a crowd at a car accident, a checkered tablecloth, clowns at a circus. He supplements this imagery with studio sessions with live models. Of the thousands of images he's taken over the years, he's used only about one-tenth in his photomontages, some over and over again, provoking the poet Frank O'Hara to write that "he explores the visual event…in much the way a poet again and again reposes his confidence in a favorite word to wring more specific qualities from it."

Each photomontage begins when Telberg spreads part of his negative library over his light box. He'll select an image that moves him and then build on it, using two enlargers, sandwiching negatives, solarizing, and more recently, dribbling developer over the paper, in search of affecting image combinations and textures. He works intuitively, almost consciously forcing his subconscious to supervise the creation of each montage.

Telberg was at first shy about circulating his images, but eventually, at the urging of a friend, took them to Edward Steichen. Steichen was enthusiastic and included him in the 1948 Museum of Modern Art exhibit "In and Out of Focus," where his montages hung with the works of Strand, Callahan, Siskind,

Mohaly-Nagy, Man Ray, and Cartier-Bresson. The same year, Telberg had his first one-person show at the Brooklyn Museum. He's exhibited extensively since.

Telberg has always said that if filmmaking had come into his life sooner, he would have been a filmmaker. "I envy that medium," he says. "I consider it the ultimate art." Cinematic sequencing is a purposeful part of Telberg's montages. "I want to hold the viewer's eye longer by suggesting that there is more. I often put images in the darker parts of the print to be discovered later. In an exhibition, I like to have the same model appear in several pictures."

In the fifties, Telberg indulged his fascination with cinema by working on several avant-garde films, including Ian Hugo's *Bells of Atlantis*. Through Hugo, Telberg met Anaïs Nin, who was intrigued by his photomontages and asked him to illustrate a new edition of her prose poem *House of Incest*. Over the course of a year, Telberg and Nin worked together, Telberg making over two hundred montages. Nin selected those she felt were most evocative of the poem. "She liked my work particularly because she saw a reaction to her work. It was very serious, very intense."

Telberg has likened his imagery to abstract poetry and has written "it comes very close to being stream of consciousness in visual form." And as a poet uses punctuation, Telberg deliberately uses certain formal elements of visual composition to manipulate viewers. "When I'm working on a picture, I'm conscious of certain aesthetic rules, like meter in poetry, like rhyme or lack of rhyme. I'm conscious of composition. It's very important for me to compose a picture that has intentional lack of balance or balance." For the same reason, Telberg experiments with matte shapes, to aid the montages' total composition and influence the way viewers see it.

But at the same time he speaks with ease of manipulating viewers, the precise words for exactly *why* he wants to manipulate them come hard. Writing in the *New Mexico Quarterly* in 1954, he says, "For some reason unknown to me I have an urge to make a certain kind of picture." I sense that almost thirty years later, the reason is just as elusive.

Telberg knows he wants his photographs to communicate distress, but he's not sure why. He'll tell you that art that expresses pain is somehow more urgent than art that does not, that someone once told him that in music the downbeat is the offbeat and is therefore more unsettling than the upbeat. But here Telberg is talking technique again, and not motive.

"The changes are so inviting," Telberg has written of his darkroom sessions, "that there is never an end—every print is work in progress and nothing is ever completed with finality because not to end is so easy." Then how does he know when to stop? With an impish grin, he says, "My wife calls me to dinner."

In other words, the alarm goes off.

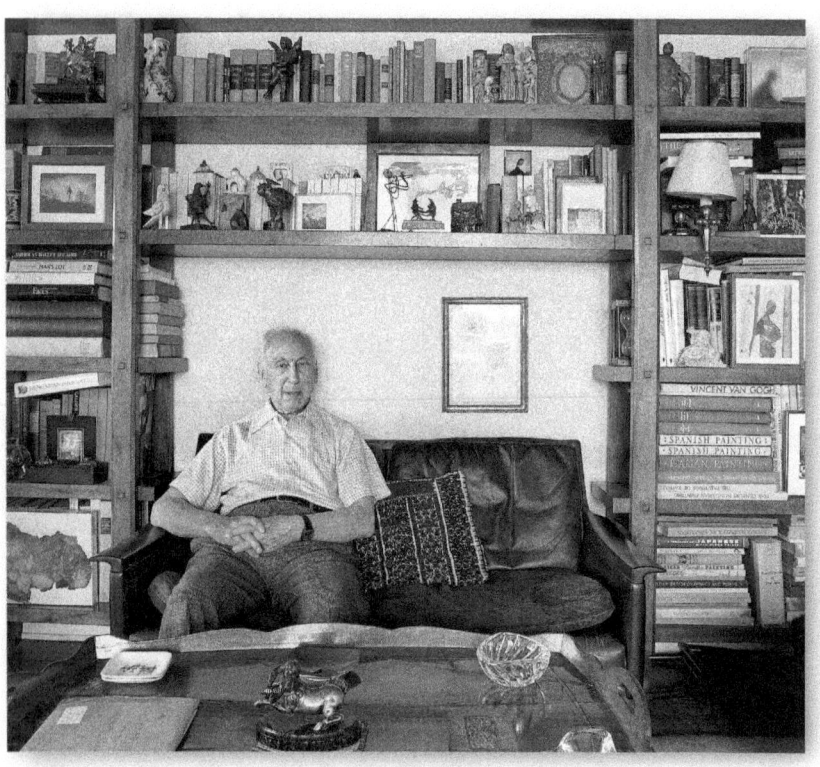

Photo by Kurt Fishback

ANDRÉ KERTÉSZ (1894–1985)

An Up and Down Life

Published September/October 1983

In 1982, the most recent of André Kertész's twenty-four books of photography, *Hungarian Memories,* was honored as one of the top photography books of the year; a vintage 1926 contact print, with the unassuming dimensions of 9 x 12 cm, sold for $15,000; France awarded him its coveted Prix de Photographie; and he was profiled in *Newsweek*. As one of the first photographers to wield a Leica, Kertész pioneered small-format photojournalism and sequential reportage and was one of the first to experiment with night photography. Cartier-Bresson and Brassai are among those who acknowledge his influence.

With these not exactly trifling credits, one would assume Kertész, now eighty-nine, to be a photographer long known and revered in the world of photography. In fact, the role of a celebrity is not unfamiliar to him; fifty years ago, he was one of Europe's most celebrated art photographers and photojournalists. Then he moved to the United States, only to discover that America, enamored of the sharp-focus precision of f/64 photography and coolly objective photojournalism, was not at all receptive to his distinctly different style. Only within the past few years has his work gained prominence here, allowing him his rightful place in the international pantheon of great pioneer photographers.

Kertész now lives in New York City, in a Fifth Avenue apartment overlooking Washington Square Park, where he has lived alone since the death of his wife Elizabeth five years ago. Pushing ninety, he's yet lucid and industrious. A hearing impediment caused by an illness he suffered shortly after his arrival in the United States makes the standard interview difficult, but he's a practiced storyteller, and little more than a shouted word is necessary to send him off on a tale. Even after almost fifty years in America, his English is still heavily punctuated with French and his native Hungarian. "I tell you my story," he says. "I made my biggest mistake in the moment I came to America. And I tell you frankly. All the best things what happened to me was in Paris and in Hungary. All the worst things happened here in America."

André Kertész was born in Budapest, Hungary, on July 2, 1894, the second of three sons. His father was a successful tradesman and one of the accouterments of the family's comfortable, middle-class existence was a camera with which family gatherings were ritually recorded. At six, he discovered his vocation. On a visit to relatives in the country, he unearthed an old magazine illustrated with intriguing woodcuts in a musty corner of the attic. "Instinct tells me maybe I can do this with photography," he says. Too proud to ask his parents to buy him a camera, he began looking at the world as if through the camera viewfinder, practicing for the time when he could buy his own. It was good education. Shortly after receiving his baccalaureate from the Academy of Commerce in 1912 and taking a job as a clerk in the stock exchange, he bought an ICA box camera with twelve 4.5 x 6 cm glass plates: "In the very first moment I had my own personal camera in my hand, I made immediately the composition perfectly right. Balance, timing, everything was right."

Kertész worked on the stock exchange during the day and printed the photos he took on weekends at night, learning developing and printing by trial and error in the darkroom he set up in the big family armoire. In those early days of photography, it was fashionable to make photographs that resembled paintings or etchings. Exposures were blurred, and prints were processed to create a diffused, "painterly" image. From the very beginning, his style rebelled against this tradition. He shunned the large-format cameras favored then for more portable smaller cameras that allowed him to capture candid poses and trained his camera on scenes few other photographers would have bothered to record: two cocks on a cobbled street, a young man snoozing open-mouthed over his morning newspaper.

When World War I started in 1914, Kertész joined the Austro-Hungarian army, taking his camera, then a Goerz Tenax, with him. Even if it hadn't been dangerous to haul a camera up to the front lines, he wasn't inclined to photograph carnage and destruction. His camera caught behind-the-lines action: six soldiers sitting in a row on a makeshift open-air latrine; a column of soldiers marching through a pastoral landscape, the curve and texture of their line harmonizing with a stand of trees in the distance; a soldier reaching to pat a peasant girl's behind during an off-duty stroll through the countryside.

After the war, in 1918, Kertész returned to Budapest and to his old job in the stock exchange. "I was unhappy," he recalls. His friends had begun to drift off to Paris—"this was the place!"—and he told his widowed mother that he too wanted to go. His mother disapproved. After all, photography was a more suitable hobby than a profession. Loathe to contradict her, Kertész stayed on, switching to a job in an agricultural office, hoping field assignments would give him more opportunities for photographing, then trying farming, an endeavor that flopped when Hungary's farms went communal.

By this time, Kertész had published a few photographs in local newspapers, and in 1923, he entered four photographs in an amateur photographers' competition. The ensuing anecdote is one he loves to tell as illustrative of photographic fashion in the early twenties and his own stubborn refusal to compromise his divergent artistic standards. When the competition's judges contacted him to say they would award him the silver medal if he would turn the photographs into bromoil prints, he told them thanks but no thanks. "The bromoil is an artificial gravure. What I give them is pure photography. I don't want to imitate nothing a la Steichen and company. Playing with the photo material is different than making the photo." In place of the medal, he received a mere diploma, but to his gratification, the prints were exhibited just as he had made them.

"Not long after, my mother decided to let me go to Paris." The deciding factor was the publication of a Kertész photograph on the cover of *Erdekes Urjsag,* an illustrated magazine that he had contributed to intermittently since 1912, when he'd taken a selection of photos to the editors for their professional criticism. "*Alors,* this worked on my mother. She said, 'My boy, you are right! This is not the place for your work.'" Kertész was off to Paris.

With savings to sustain him for at least six months, Kertész, then thirty-one, rented a garret apartment in Montparnasse and happily took to the street with his camera, shooting what he liked. He began to frequent the Café du Dome, a favored gathering place of artists and intellectuals who met to swap achievements.

Artists began asking Kertész for prints from which to paint, which he gladly gave them, undoubtedly influencing their work. They, in turn, influenced his. He continued to pursue candid, humanistic scenes, but with an even more discerning eye to graphic composition, and began to work seriously on the surreal distortions he had begun making in Hungary. His reputation spread, and by the end of 1926, strangers began to purchase prints. On March 12, 1927, fourteen months after his arrival in Paris, his first one-man show was mounted at the Sacre du Printemps gallery.

Among the artists and writers with whom Kertész associated then were Mondrian, Colette, Brancusi, and Chagall, all of whom he immortalized in now-famous portraits, as well as Brassaï, whom he met shortly after his arrival. Of the latter, Kertész remembers, "He was an excellent writer, excellent sculptor, excellent designer, philosopher too, but not interested in photography. There were daily money difficulties for artists and intellectuals then, and he was struggling. So one day I tell him, 'This is absolutely ridiculous. You are an intelligent man. You should begin photographing. With the money for the photo, you can paint or sculpt.' *Mais non.* He don't wanted. So I tell him, 'You come with me, you want or you don't want.' He came with me, and I give him every possible instruction, technically and from an artistic point of view too, including the night photos. I made the first one in 1914. Ten years later, it was my first cover."

Kertész anticipated photographic fashion by championing the small-format 4.5 x 6 cm cameras over the cumbersome large-format cameras most other photographers used, and when the 35mm Leica was introduced, he was naturally one of the first purchasers. Using the lightweight camera to photograph what one observer described as "the significant background of world-shaking events," he began freelancing for Europe's top magazines and periodicals, including the *Frankfurter Illustrierte, Le Matin, Le Nazionale de Fiorenze* and the *London Times.* Museums and libraries began buying his prints, and in the years between 1933 and 1936, he published three collections of photographs—*Les Enfants, Paris Vu Par André Kertész,* and *Nos Amis les Betes.* In 1928, Lucien Vogel began publication of *Journal Vu,* an illustrated magazine on which *Life* was later modeled, and Kertész was its star photographer. Alexander Liberman, who went on to become one of the most successful publishing potentates in history, and under whom Kertész would later work at Conde Nast Publications, was then fresh out of art school, working in the art department.

At the height of his European success, in 1933, Kertész married Elizabeth Sali, whom he'd known in Budapest, and who, like many young people with artistic inclinations, had arrived in Paris in 1931 to become part of the international community of artists. She ultimately devoted herself to him; theirs was a lifelong love affair. She figures affectionately in many of his photographs, and most of his books are dedicated to her.

Soon thereafter, in 1936, Kertész and Elizabeth arrived in New York at the invitation of Ernie Prince, head of the Keystone Agency. Prince had lured Kertész away from Paris for what he thought would be a single sabbatical year spent in America doing reportage. The day before he left, a State Department representative called on him to offer him French citizenship for artistic merit, a rare honor. Kertész thanked him emotionally, offered his regrets that he was leaving the country, and promised to accept the award officially on his return. Circumstances would prevent him from keeping that promise. "I made my biggest mistake the moment I accepted this one year," he says bitterly, "Details, better if you don't know. The most dirtiest things happened, one right after the other."

It began one evening shortly after his arrival, when Kertész received a call from Dr. Agha, then art director at Conde Nast, who was eager to work with him. Kertész told him that if he wanted anything, he should contact Prince. "Ernie Prince?" asked Agha. "André, I hope he hasn't cheated you." Prince, it turned out, had a reputation for publishing other photographers' work under his name. Sure enough, several photographers appeared in *Look* with Prince's credit. Moreover, the reportage Kertész had been promised had turned out to be "ordinary commercial work and advertising photography. *Malheureusement*, in the time I discovered this, in the third month, my money was not in my hand, and I couldn't return to France."

There followed a numbing series of bewildering personal and professional disappointments. When Beaumont Newhall, the Museum of Modern Art's young curator, asked Kertész to contribute several of his photographs, including some of his nude distortions, to the museum's first international exhibition of photography, he was delighted. "I was very glad he wanted to use. The distortions I did only in the last three of four years, and Paris accepted nicely. Germany accepted, and they began going around Central Europe. I hoped America would like them too." But Newhall felt there was too much blatant nudity in the photographs, and asked Kertész to tone down the sex. "He said, 'With the sex is pornography what you did. Without the sex is art.'" In the end, Kertész complied. "I felt completely confused. The representative of the big Museum of Modern Art in America talking this way? And so I give in."

Kertész experienced a different form of censorship from American magazines. In 1937, *Life, Journal Vu's* American progeny, was in its first year of publication, and Kertész went over to pay a friendly visit. *Life's* staff greeted him enthusiastically; they knew his work well. For *Life's* purposes, though, they told him he talked too much with his pictures. "This is a mistake!" This is an illustrated magazine. You *should* talk with illustrations." But *Life* had an editor to elucidate the photographs through captions. "*Alors!* I make document and talk too. *Comme* reporter I want to talk. I *should* talk."

The idea that photojournalism should be objective was something that Kertész would come up against repeatedly. "I feel I have no place in America. Documenting is not for me. I try to do some, but it was impossible. Everybody had two cents. Do this. Do that. In Paris, we did not do it this way. In the *real* reportage style, you read the article and go out with your personality. Not everybody two-centing."

Kertész was stuck in the United States. Not only was his money gone, but World War II had started, and as a Hungarian, he was considered an enemy alien. He was fingerprinted and restricted to photographing indoors. "In street with camera, I was spy."

To earn a living, Kertész made "ordinary commercial photographs" for *Harper's, Vogue, Town & Country, Colliers,* and *House Beautiful.* But one month, he found himself short on cash and unable to pay the rent for his residential hotel rooms. "I lived in this hotel for two years. And I paid regularly. The manager knows me. I tell him, look, maybe this month I am three or four days late with rent. This was maybe eight or nine days *before* the end of the month. I have the right to stay to the end, but that night I come home, and the door was locked."

Abruptly, without preparation or plan, Kertész and his wife found themselves literally on the street. As they stood wondering what to do, he began to feel nauseous and dizzy. Then he collapsed. "I lost myself. Elizabeth began desperately asking for help. It was eleven o'clock. There were a few people on the street, but no one helped. Around midnight, after one hour, slowly, slowly, I became stronger."

Kertész had a rare syndrome called Meniere's disease, and he lost most of his hearing during those hours on the street. He continued to experience spontaneous dizzy spells for almost three years. He told no one of the illness and kept on taking assignments, never knowing if he would be able to complete them. Fortunately, the spells came only during nonworking hours, and he was able to keep his illness to himself.

"In the time this happened, the doctor was telling me no more darkroom. If I go in, the red light makes me dizzy. You can imagine. I was desperate." Kertész began sending his film out for processing, but was invariably unhappy with the results." After I became a little better, I try cheating the doctor. I try for fifteen years. Go in the darkroom and try and try and try." Eventually, he found Igor Bakht, a printer with whom he has now worked for seventeen years. He pays Bakht the highest compliment a photographer can offer a printer: "He is doing exactly what I would do."

Kertész continued freelancing, and in 1946, he had his last one-man show for almost twenty years at the Art Institute of Chicago. It attracted virtually no critical attention. "I tell you," he says, speaking retrospectively of his lack of support from the American artistic community, "If Newhall exhibit, if Steichen exhibit, then maybe I could have come out. But in America in the time I came, the biggest thing was f/64. You know what is f/64? I explicate— f/64 is perfect technique. But it's like writing. You can learn to handwrite beautifully, but what's more important is what you are writing. f/64—this means the minimum was the maximum for America." Feeling drained and defeated, he signed an exclusive contract with Conde Nast publications in 1949. "It was not interesting what I did for Conde Nast—just illustration," he dismisses the next thirteen years.

World War II had uprooted the *Journal Vu* staff, depositing both Lucien Vogel and Alexander Liberman in New York, where Conde Nast gave his old friend Vogel a small office and the title of advisor and Liberman the job of art director. He replaced a recalcitrant Dr. Agha. "In the moment he became art director, he called," says Kertész. "'André, can we working together?'" I told him, "Alex, you know very well I am reporter. This is not for me." But Liberman was persuasive. Kertész took the job of revamping *House & Garden*. "You understand French?" he asks. "It was *merde*."

"I changed *House & Garden* in one year. Then the other magazines began calling for me. My idea was gaining some money, some independence, and going back in Paris. I brought it up and they said, 'André, please don't go. We give you contract.' And I was there thirteen years. It was, believe me, suffering."

Kertész photographed for all of the Conde Nast publications, even trying his hand at fashion for *Vogue*. Meanwhile, he watched Liberman succumb to the pressures of directing consumer publications, which, to attract the advertisers who support them, must cater to mainstream tastes. "All my respect for Alex," he says. "He tried to do intelligent, honest, artistic, and literary work. He tried months and months. He became sick—sick and nervous. And the moment came when he decided: America wants the other side, so I do the other side. And he don't have the courage to tell me, ' André change too.'

"Several times he give me assignments. I did the subject in a way I thought was sensitive and interesting. When I presented the work, he say, 'André, very nice. But can I ask you please go back. And make an ordinary presentation.' I ask him, 'Alex, why? Why send me? Anybody from the street can do this.'" Liberman quietly insisted.

By the early sixties, Kertész was thoroughly frustrated with his work for Conde Nast. During that time, he went into the hospital for an operation, and in the course of a lengthy recuperation period, he came to a decision. "I think over my American existence, and I decided I don't want to give in, even if I have nothing to eat. Is more important with this son of a bitch life to hold on and do what *I* want, honestly, humanly, artistically. In cents and dollars, I have a difficult life, not making the big money a la Avedon and company. It was more important for me to be honestly artist."

Kertész terminated his contract with Conde Nast in 1962 and began concentrating on selling his own work, this time around with positive results. In 1963, he landed a one-man show at Long Island University in New York, and in 1964, the Museum of Modern Art's John Szarkowski, impressed with the abundance of fine photographs Kertész brought to show him, mounted a one-man show at Museum of Modern Art that met with critical acclaim. He's since exhibited internationally and is represented by galleries through the United States. His prints sell for a minimum of $1,000.

One evening in the early seventies, Kertész encountered Liberman at a Museum of Modern Art reception in Lord Snowden's honor. "'André,' he asked me, are you still photographing?' 'Yes,' I tell him. 'I am *only* photographing.'"

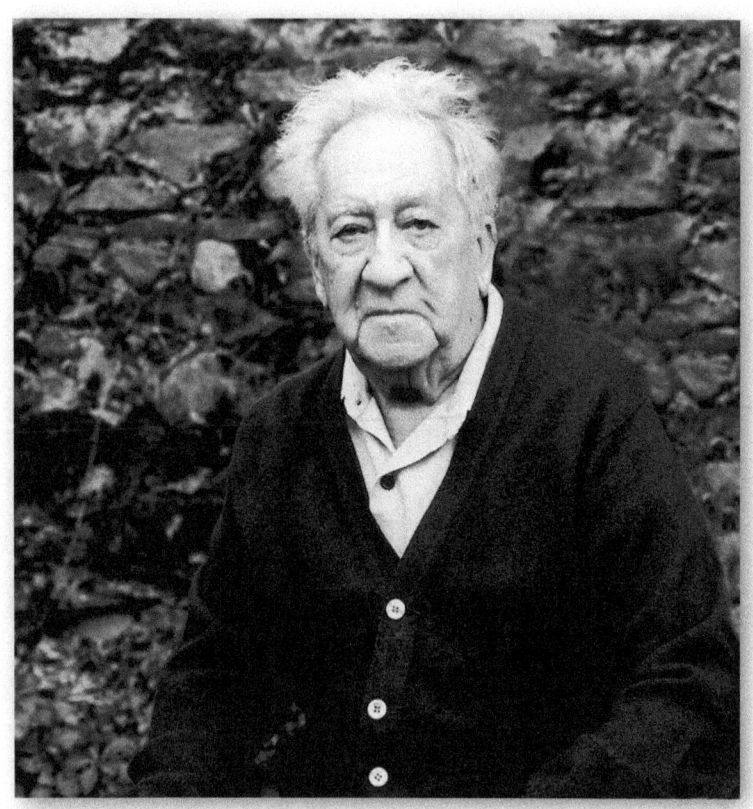

Photo by Neal Rantoul

Conflicting Rhythms

Published March/April 1984

Photography wasn't his first choice among the arts, but at age twenty-six, when Aaron Siskind finally took a camera into his hands, he knew he'd found his medium. His subsequent contribution to photography, both as a photographer and a teacher, has been substantial, as has been his influence on several generations of visual artists—painters as well as photographers.

Siskind has published several collections of photographs, including *Places* and *Harlem Document*, and is the subject of a critical biography by Carl Chiarenza, *Aaron Siskind: Pleasures and Terrors*. At seventy-nine, he continues to photograph, based from his comfortable two-story home on a quiet, residential street in Providence, Rhode Island.

JB: Why did you become a photographer?

AS: I wanted to be a writer and a musician, and I was an abject failure at both of them. I was given a camera as a belated wedding present in 1930, and it soon came to mean a great deal to me. It gave me a boost because I felt such a sense of failure then. I'd made a bad marriage. My wife, whom I'd known since childhood, was very sick mentally. I was really in a very bad way and felt a great need to be successful at something creative. I began by taking pictures at various odd moments and did that on my own for about two years.

JB: How did you become involved with the Photo League?

AS: In 1932 or 1933, in the depths of the Depression, I wandered in and saw an exhibition that really moved me, so I joined. I soon learned that the Photo League was related to the Communist Party. They kept trying to convert me. I was already politically sophisticated because I was brought up as a socialist. As a child, I was a member of the Junior Young People's Socialist League, and I was a little radical in high school. All that made me politically aware. I subsequently lost interest in politics when I took up with music and poetry.

The Photo League renewed my interest in politics. After I joined, I went to the Worker's School and took classes, but never joined the Party. At that time, though, everybody was involved in the radical movement because it seemed like it was a ray of hope. That's why during the years when they were investigating these people, they turned up so-called Communist connections everywhere because almost everybody belonged to an organization like the Film and Photo League or the Artists Union. I was an active member in the Photo League. I took charge of exhibitions, put them together, and shipped them around to union halls and places like that. In 1936, we formed a real production group—the Feature Group—that met regularly and kept minutes.

JB: What did the Photo League teach you about photography?

AS: In the beginning, I learned a lot of simple basic things. I didn't know anything. The people there helped me set up a darkroom. We held regular critiquing sessions that I learned a lot from.

JB: The group was devoted exclusively to documentary photography, wasn't it?

AS: That's right. Almost every other kind of photography was a hateful thing to the people in the Photo League. There were only a few photographers working outside the group who they admired. These were naturally people who had done documentary work and were either apolitical or pro-political, like Paul Strand. But if you were a good documentary photographer yet hated all kinds of political movements and organizations—like Walker Evans—you were out.

JB: Wasn't the Photo League's aim to make propagandistic documentary photographs?

AS: They had a motto: "Art is a weapon of the working class."

JB: How did you feel about that?

AS: I was willing to investigate it. We spent a lot of time examining the relationship between a picture and an idea, what you can say with a picture. We made several "documents"—studies of various segments of New York life. The big one was the Harlem Document. These weren't really propagandistic pictures. We did furnish our photographs to some left magazines, but we also sold them to *Fortune* and *Look*. We just wanted to promote a larger understanding of the plight of certain segments of society. There were people involved, though, who were very political, and who would consciously use these pictures for political purposes.

JB: What were your conclusions after exploring the Photo League's theories?

AS: My conclusion was to get the hell out. The atmosphere there was very intolerant, and I could not long tolerate a situation where directives were handed down to you, where self-motivation was absent. I couldn't stand that—not in the making of anything you call art. It was essentially a very tight political organization. Those members who held different opinions were always thrown out and ostracized. If you didn't believe [he makes a slashing motion across his throat], zingo. If you disagreed, zingo.

JB: Did your involvement in the Photo League ever come back to haunt you during the McCarthy witch-hunts?

AS: No, I was never brought to task for being a member. But I was only a member, and that doesn't prove you're a Communist, although someone told me he saw a dossier on me at the FBI, and they have me down as a Communist.

A well-known photographer and very good friend of mine, Max Yavno, *was* a Party member. He was president of the Photo League for a while. They would never make me the president, although I was ten times more active than he was, simply because I wasn't a Communist. When he went into the army, he wanted to get into the officer's training program, and they put him on the carpet. The FBI came around and interviewed me because at one time we lived together. You know, it was funny. If we were together, it was me people would take for the Communist. I looked more like a Jew-boy Communist, you know? Max, in comparison, looked like a bourgeois. He was always meticulously dressed and his shoes were always beautifully shined.

JB: Didn't you live with Yavno in a part of Greenwich Village where a number of artists had congregated, artists whose work and ideas subsequently affected the direction your work took?

AS: Yes, and what was interesting was that just as I became disillusioned, a lot of artists who were members of the Artists Union and so forth were becoming equally disillusioned. They didn't like being dictated to either, and so they got out, one after the other. This seemed to set them free. Then, when the war began, European artists began immigrating to New York—wonderful artists—and they had considerable influence. As American artists acquired self-confidence, they began asserting themselves, changing their styles, experimenting. That was the beginning of the abstract expressionist movement, which made America a leader in the world of art. I became a part of it later on after I had done a little work on my own. I had a show at one of the leading avant-garde galleries, the Egan gallery, in 1947, and three more shows in quick succession.

JB: Your abstract photographs are often compared to the work of artists like de Kooning, Kline, and Pollock, and it's generally assumed that they influenced you. But didn't your work in that vein actually precede theirs?

AS: Some of it did, some of it did not. People are so uptight about influences—who did it before the other guy, where you got your ideas from, and all of that. But no artist exists by himself. Everybody gets ideas from someone else. This is the nature of all cultural acts, which have within themselves an endless history. My photographs have within themselves a particular history. Exactly what that history *is* is not easy to dig out, even for me. That's for a historian like Carl Chiarenza. These things are very intricate. What most people don't realize is that the whole process is wonderful. I had real contact with other artists, and I was receiving what they had in a very live way—rejecting some things, using others. I did show at the Egan gallery three years before Franz Kline, with whom I was very close. De Kooning had his first show a couple of years after I did. I don't know how important those facts are.

JB: Your meetings with these artists were informal more often than not, taking place in restaurants and taverns like the Cedar Bar. When you met, did you criticize each other's work per se, or were your meetings more an interchange of ideas?

AS: It was really more an interchange of ideas, but there was also a lot of criticism. There was always a lot of talk in the studios, and, as you say, in the bars. A *lot* of talk. I remember that in all that time I was fairly silent. My background in the visual arts was not very strong. My background was in poetry, literature, and music. I found a great deal of satisfaction in making pictures, and I was successful because I was using my background in literature and in poetry and music to do it. Then, little by little, as I got to know more about art, the influence of the other visual artists, like painters, became stronger and stronger.

JB: How were you using music and poetry in your photography?

AS: I found, in the early years, that I was organizing my abstract pictures rhythmically. As an example of what I'm talking about, I remember trying to get a particular student then to make a picture that way, not simply as a rendition of a subject. I told her, go out and get going rhythmically, and then little by little you'll find that what is visual and what is rhythmic will come together—in terms of accents, of longs and shorts. So that's where the music went, not only in a generally inspirational way but in terms of rhythm and repetitions that can be expressed visually.

Now, poetry was a little bit deeper and subtler. I saw I was beginning to make pictures that were ambiguous, that had multiple meanings. I remember pondering that—asking myself, what does this mean? Why do you do this? The answer I came up with is we just don't see simply. I'm seeing that and seeing that [he points to the periphery]. And at the same time, I'm remembering, drawing on memory. That's the kind of picture I wanted to make—a picture that has meaning, or meanings, and depth. That's what poetry is.

I think the thing that I've contributed to photography is that I began to bring the other arts in in a very organic way. Later on, I began to bring the other visual arts into my prints and influence other artists as well. Painters began to come to photography to get ideas. After a while, it got to be so intertwined, flowing back and forth, that it would be very difficult to determine where anything came from. But that's wonderful.

In the seventies, to commemorate and honor this interchange, I worked for three years on my "Homage to Franz Kline." I tell my students that and it's a big shock to them because they look at me and see somebody original and special, and then I talk about the community of artists—how wonderful this thing is to be in contact with all these wonderful minds. I say this is a thing to celebrate. You *celebrate* influences. You *celebrate* relationships.

JB: One photographer with whom you're constantly paired in print and at exhibitions is Harry Callahan. Yet your work is very different.

AS: Yes, our work is very, very different. The only similarity is that our photographs are simply just pictures, and we both work very economically. The statement is clear and clean. His you can understand. Mine you can't understand. But it *looks* clear—sparse, you know? There were very few photographers, and since we were teaching together, people always thought of us together and showed us together in Europe and all over the country. But I think our relationship has endured because our work is so different and our personalities are so different. We're not competitive.

JB: How did you meet?

AS: I met Harry in New York through a mutual photographer friend. Later on, I went out to Chicago, and we went out and did some shooting together in an automobile graveyard. The next time we got together, I think, was in Black Mountain, where we taught together one summer. He had been running the photography program at the Chicago Institute of Design, and he had been asking me to come out.

JB: He asked you a number of times, didn't he?

AS: Yeah, and I didn't want to leave New York. Then I quit my elementary school teaching job and thought I'd become a *real* photographer.

JB: What made you decide to do that?

AS: I had just taken my first sabbatical in twenty-three years. I was on the Vineyard where I always went in the summer, walking with a friend of mine, Jane Teller, a sculptor whom I'd known for many years. We sat down to rest, and I took a postcard out of my pocket to show her. It was an offer to teach photography one day a week at Trenton Junior College in New Jersey for $1,000 a year. I said to her, "You know, Janie, if I had the assurance of another $1,000, I think I'd quit my teaching job, but my parents are getting old, and I have to contribute something to the household, so I have to have a decent income." And so Janie, who's fairly well off, said, "Aaron, if all you need is $1,000 to do what you want to do I'll give you $1,000." So

I took the job. A week later, I went down to the Board of Education and resigned. I was forty-six or forty-seven and had taught elementary school ever since I got out of college.

JB: When did you take Callahan up on his offer?

AS: I worked in Trenton for two years. All that time, Harry kept writing me. He knew that I was just the right guy for him, that I knew how to teach and had done documentary work. So I went out there, and we worked together for ten years. Then he came here to Providence, to the Rhode Island School of Design. I stayed on at the Institute of Design for another ten years, and when they threw me out of there—I'd reached retirement age—he invited me to come here. So we taught here together, and we're still very close friends.

JB: How did the celebrity that you and your work acquired in the seventies affect you?

AS: After such a long time without it, it just made me feel better. We were nowhere in the fifties and sixties. I couldn't make a living from my photography. I was selling pictures for ten dollars and twenty dollars. Photography was growing then. I had a lot of graduate students who were doing interesting photography, I was showing more—all those things are nice, you know? But I can't remember ever being able to get through a month on my salary in the sixties. I always had to do a portrait job or even photograph paintings. I did a lot of that. Callahan and I would do any job we could get. I remember once we got a job with the *Encyclopedia Britannica Jr.*, making pictures illustrating experiments—like how water is absorbed by a sponge. We were both lousy at it, although he was a little better than me. We called ourselves Dumb Photographers Inc., and we got twenty-five dollars a shot.

Then in 1966, everything changed for me. I had a brother I hardly talked to. He was an engineer who had written books on engineering and taught at Purdue University. He died, and I inherited $50,000 from him because he didn't leave a will. The first thing I did was to borrow $10,000 against my inheritance from the bank that was handling the will. Then I had $10,000. I bought my Eames chair, a new hi-fi system, a Volvo, and we had a little left, so we went to Europe. I finally got a Guggenheim then too, and that helped. From then on, everything has been very nice.

JB: I assume that's when you began traveling all over the world, which brings me to the concept of "place" in your photographs. Your monograph is called *Places*, and you've returned to the same places time and time again to photograph—Corfu, Mexico, and Peru. Yet one would never recognize those places in your photographs.

AS: That's a very interesting question, and I think about it a lot. What effect does place have on what I'm photographing, and are my pictures really about that place? Well, they're not *really* about that place, but I can't figure out what else they're about. When I did the Franz Kline series, I did it in three countries. If you look at the pictures, they're quite different. Whether my being there and how I feel when I'm there has any kind of effect, I can't tell you definitely, although everyone will say that logically it must have. Certainly, everything I photographed was either touched or made by the people who were there. Is that significant? Does it show? I don't know. At the time, I was interested not only in recording it but also converting it for my own purposes to what I wanted it to say for me. So the effect of place is very dubious, or certainly indefinite. I think that what comes into play more than anything is what I was talking about before—art and my relationship to art and artists and the history of art. That's what makes me see what I see, and it gives me the means by which I can translate it. A lot of people talk about my removing myself from the world. They're wrong for many reasons.

JB: Removing yourself from the world in the sense that your photographs are abstract?

AS: Yes. They're wrong because I'm relating to the history of art and how people have been thinking for many, many centuries, all over the world. I am in contact with the world in my way, but in order to make contact with that world while I'm working, I have to remove myself from the world of events. When you're making a picture, you have to be alone with what you're making the picture with. You're having a conversation with that stuff, see? And you are a very, very complicated person at that moment. You have all the history of art in you. You've got the pictures you made yesterday or fifteen minutes ago. And you have to isolate yourself from the traffic noise, from the people, from everything. Then you get your intensity. Even photojournalists have to do that. They'll knock down people, kick things out of the way, and the more intense they are, the better their pictures are. And what about the people who are there? You think about them, feel them, see them, but not when you're making the picture. They're there, but in a kind of subtle, insinuating way.

JB: What kinds of cameras have you used over the years?

AS: I haven't had a great many cameras or changed formats very often. For the first ten years, I worked with an inexpensive Voigtlander Avis I bought in 1932 for twenty-eight dollars. It was wonderful. Then I dropped it, and it broke, so I bought another to replace it. That one was stolen while I was living with Max Yavno. His reaction was, "Thank God! Now you can get a decent camera." I bought a slightly better one, an inexpensive Linhof, secondhand. With the Linhof, I went to 4 x 5. I used that for many, many years, and I still have it. In the last ten to fifteen years I've been using a single lens Rollei. I use it as a view camera. It's too heavy to hold in my hands.

I use an enlarger like anybody else's. I print my pictures straight. I don't fuss. Harry and I have never fussed. I often say to students there isn't anything I know about making a picture that you can't learn in a year's time. When my assistant Judy prints a picture of mine, I say I want it like this, and she does it. You can't tell hers from mine. Sometimes hers come out even a little better than mine. I print the early stages of things. I do the proofing and the first print so that she'll have something to work from.

JB: Is there a film you prefer?

AS: No one more than any other. I keep buying different brands, but there's very little difference, although each one has slightly different characteristics. As for the paper, Ilford is making one with more silver in it now, Galerie. That's what we use sometimes.

JB: A few years ago, you mentioned to an interviewer that you were playing around with color.

AS: I've tried, yeah. On my last trip to Peru, I did black-and-white and color. I haven't gotten anything great yet. There's something wrong in my perception of color, I think. I don't have any idea what the picture's going to turn out like when I shoot it. I know the shapes and so forth, but not how dense it's going to be, how much contrast is going to be in it, how the different colors will finally work out in configuration. I also have a habit of working in diffused light, and that's very bad for color. So I haven't had much luck.

JB: One final question. Religious icons are thematic to your work. Are you religious?

AS: Not really, and maybe that's why it's so important to my work. I take the rational view of life. There's no life after death. I'm not big enough to comprehend a God. I love church architecture. I love church music. But I think the guy's talking a lot of nonsense. Now that's what I consciously believe. But I really am another kind of person. I hear music, I cry. I see an event, and I'm just melted. I love to sit in churches. When I was a young man, that's all I used to do—sit and read in a church. It's *hard* to read in church. The light's bad. So what do I do? I make icons, photographs that contain various elements that can be used for inspiration and contemplation. What's happening is that I'm taking this real inner conflict and resolving it in a picture. That's the source of the tensions in my pictures. They're there because I'm resolving, or trying to resolve, inner conflicts.

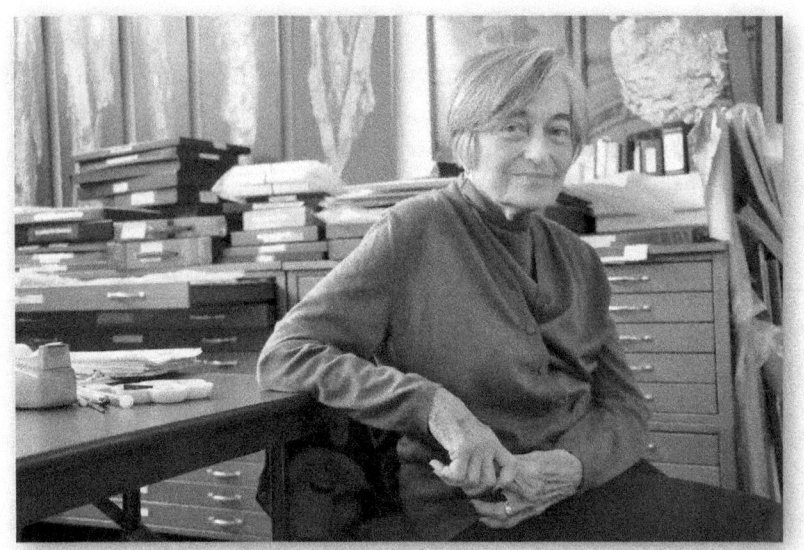
Photo by Chester Alamo-Costello

BARBARA CRANE (1928–)

Fresh Angles

Published July/August 1984

J ust because Chicago's Barbara Crane watches television while she works in her darkroom, don't think she's not serous. A few years back, she started lifting weights, not because it was all the rage, but because she figured some extra muscle would make it easier for her to tote her 8 x 10 view camera. Others take her seriously too. For example, she's the first living photographer to have her work published in book form by Arizona's Center for Creative Photography.

Over the past thirty years, Crane has worked in everything from Polaroid to platinum; her imagery ranges from single to multiple, abstract to representational. She's made prints that cover the side of a building and prints of a more traditional size. All this variety makes her work tough to pigeonhole. But there is a coherent method to what may seem at a glance to be madness.

JB: Is it true that you have a television in your darkroom?

BC: Yes, with a red gel on it. The darkroom can start to feel very isolating, especially after many years of working in it all day and not knowing whether the sun's out or if it's raining. It's better than listening to music for me because it's more as if people are there. Sometimes, it can get distracting though. I've been known to burn-in on a print and then discover, when I put it in the developer, that there are all these dark spots and no picture. That's because I got hooked on watching something. Otherwise, it makes the tedium much easier to bear.

JB: Your photos are both abstract and representational, and you seem to alternate regularly between the two. Why is that?

BC: Actually, it has a lot to do with summer and winter. In the winter, I stay indoors and do the more abstract, manipulative work. In the summer, I love to be outside and in an urban setting. I love crowds of people of all nationalities. But over and above that, I feel the need to be in touch with people. As I mentioned, the darkroom can be isolating, and photographing people helps keep me away from that isolation. Then too, there's the intellectual side of me that needs fulfillment. One inclination balances the other, and they keep me from going stale in either direction.

JB: Is there a unifying concept?

BC: Well, the seasons cycle my work as far as my whereabouts go, but I tend to stick with one basic concept regardless of what I'm photographing. What's unifying about the work I've been doing these last three or four years is that I've only worked close-up with a wide-angle lens. I can't jump back and forth on basic visual issues. It takes me about three years to inch my way along to clarity on a new concept or idea. If I didn't teach and just worked on the idea, it wouldn't go much faster, because creative growth can't be speeded up. It demands time for rumination when you're unaware—at a subliminal level.

JB: Where do your ideas come from?

BC: My own work, mostly, sometimes other mediums. For some of the sequence work that was based on monotony, I was listening to American Indian music. I'm not a regular symphony-goer, but I went one day purposefully to see what I could gain from the music. I have sequence pictures that are directly related to that experience. I could never get ideas from other people's photography.

Mostly, I get my ideas from my mistakes, and it takes time to tune in to an accident. I took an SX70 flash picture of my little granddaughter.

I don't know why, but her whole head came out totally, ghostly white. About a year later—this past summer—I started doing pictures of people's heads, and there are two reasons why I washed them out. Firstly, because it fascinated me, I kept that little SX70 picture taped on the wall as a reminder. I knew my patterns well enough to know that I would deal with that some time. Then, Polaroid Corporation sent me Polachrome, which is a 35mm slide material you put in a regular 35mm camera. It has a lot of grain and it certainly isn't as smooth and beautiful a film as Kodachrome. But it was a challenge to see if I could do something exciting with that material. The picture that was a mistake gave me an idea about how to manipulate the material to make it work for me. I always work that way. I try to figure out what it is about a mistake that's wonderful, and then I use it.

JB: In addition to teaching and your art photography, you've also taken on some commercial accounts. How does that fit in with everything else?

BC: Yes, it's important to me to keep my feet outside of the teaching field, in the so-called real world. That's why I photographed buildings for the Chicago Commission on History and Architectural Landmarks for six years and why I've done murals for corporations like Baxter Travenol Labs. I didn't make a whole lot of money on those murals. The corporation gave me creative license, and when that is allowed, you spend a lot more time on your work than you would if it was just another freelance job.

I would do more of those if they came up. There's one in the Standard Oil building that's twenty-four feet long. It was designed for a long, narrow space and is a study in what I call controlled chaos. I figure I made thirty-seven cents an hour on that one. My assistant made a lot more money than I did. But I was able to investigate a new concept with that work. It's a very unusual piece. I don't know of anything else like it.

JB: Could you tell me more about it?

BC: It's called "Chicago Epic." The mural has thirty-eight 4 x 5 negatives as the structure. The rest is a film collage of people, signs, buses, and trains. There's a photo of me in it with my tripod. I figured that if Renaissance artists could put themselves into their paintings—in mob scenes in the piazza or whatever—why not me? And I needed something to tie all this together in a whimsical way, so I thought pigeons! Chicago's got a lot of pigeons. So I laid flat in the grass in Grant Park, and my assistant spread birdseed all around me. The pigeons came and ate, then she'd run at them, and they'd fly up. As they flew up, I photographed. That proof sheet by itself is a wonderful sequence. I never planned to use it as a single image, although I did a lot of pictures that used a whole roll of film for the purpose of making one picture. You know, pigeons are soft! And these were pretty considerate…I didn't get too dirty at all.

JB: Speaking of getting dirty, when did you first take up photography?

BC: In 1948. But I have to qualify that because there were eight years from 1952 to 1960 when all my darkroom equipment was packed up and I primarily raised a family. I was an art history major in college, and I had to learn to do photographic reproductions of paintings. That's what really got me started. Before that, I used to help my father in the darkroom. He was an amateur and was basically only interested in how sharp his lens was. When I was fourteen or fifteen, I helped him down in the basement making prints and stuff. But in college— that's when I knew it was the only thing I wanted to do.

JB: It must have been difficult, then, to pack away your enlarger.

BC: Yeah, sure, and there was a lot of resentment. I packed it away when we moved—from New York back to Chicago. I was pregnant with my second child. The enlarger just never got unpacked. Had we not moved, I probably wouldn't have quit photographing. After all, I continued to work even after my first child was born. But I think it was fortuitous too because I went back to work really motivated.

JB: Why the resentment?

BC: I was itching to get back to work, but when I had kids, they were my responsibility in totality. These days, men aren't so chauvinistic. They take part in the family more. But I also think that if I had kept photographing there would've been a lot of conflict: Was I giving enough time to my kids? Or was I just dabbling in my photography? You can't give your all to both of them. In the end, it all worked out very well.

JB: When you finally did take up photography in earnest, you began by studying with Aaron Siskind at the Chicago Institute of Design. How did that come about?

BC: Well, in 1960, I went back to taking pictures. All I knew how to do was portraiture, so I did children's and business executives' portraits for four years until it stopped being a challenge. I didn't know any photographers socially, but I visited galleries regularly. I had been following Aaron Siskind's work since 1949.

I was pretty much developing in isolation. The only lessons in photography I ever had were in college when I had to learn to do those reproductions—which I never learned to do too well.

JB: So you took a portfolio of your portraits to Aaron Siskind?

BC: Yes, and he said, "Why don't you go to graduate school?" I said, "Don't be silly." He said, "Well, I don't take any private students." All those years, I had liked his sense of abstraction and his strong sense of form. I had come to recognize that I had a strong and natural sense of form too. I really wanted to work with him, so the next morning I called him and said, "How do I register?"

I had been starved for the company of people who thought in visual, abstract ways, who were in tune with that whole visual world and found it exciting. I started teaching right away at New Trier, the high school I attended as a teenager, and so I didn't spend a whole lot of time at the Institute. But my mind was like a sponge after having been isolated all those years, so when I was there, I soaked it all up. It was very exciting.

JB: The program that you instituted at New Trier generated a lot of controversy, didn't it?

BC: Yes, because a lot of the assignments I gave were Bauhaus-oriented. I *still* think that's a very good method for moving someone's visual education along quickly.

JB: How were they Bauhaus-oriented?

BC: The exercises were formalistic. They were visually structured with emphasis on exploration. It works very well. Witness the fact that some of those high-school students are still photographing, doing exciting work. They still contact me. It's a route to open a lot of doors that get closed in the primary grades when you learn how to draw a turkey for Thanksgiving. But it was somewhat programmed, and there were people who felt that you couldn't program art. Nobody knows what's really good or isn't good, and what's in one day is out the next. It worked though. Even now, I never tell my students how many pictures to make, just to keep working until they've made something wonderful.

JB: Besides Aaron Siskind, who do you number among your most important influences?

BC: There are many people who've been supportive and influential. Paul Vanderbilt has been very close to me. I trust that man's mind. He's a wonderful person and has a great background in photography. He was Roy Stryker's editor, plus he's a photographer himself. He's always right on the button as far as recognizing which of my pictures are strong on multilevels and which are fresh. He's very, very interested in fresh pictures, but at the same time, they have to have emotional content, be playful, and have a sense of abstraction—you know, the whole ball of wax. He's meant a lot to me both personally and for his value system. Ansel Adams has also been very supportive.

JB: How so? His concerns seem very different from yours.

BC: Yes, and for a long time I didn't understand why he liked my work. I eventually found out. He liked the originality. I once showed him some pictures and he said, "See, there are still a lot of new things that can be done in photography."

JB: You called him in 1968 in Big Sur and said you wanted to meet him.

BC: Yes. Other people had said that they'd done it, and when I was in California, I decided to try it too. He was wonderful, although he did get me drunk on hot sake in a Japanese restaurant. But he liked my pictures. Just knowing Ansel has opened a lot of doors for me.

JB: It seems that Imogen Cunningham was also very important to you.

BC: Well, here was a woman doing her thing. I went to Mills College in California, and she used to do publicity photographs for the school. I didn't have the nerve to introduce myself then. Subsequently, I used to visit her in San Francisco, and I even helped her retouch pictures once for her retrospective show when she was eighty-nine. But she had a family, and she still did her thing. It's women who have given me that kind of hope—whether or not I knew them.

JB: What about Aaron Siskind? How did studying with him—being in such close contact with his ideas, his work, and his personality—affect your own work?

BC: Aaron was a very good catalyst for a group. There were five of us in the graduate program then. He didn't say much, but he would get the group working on each other. You never knew why he picked up one of your pictures. You'd start thinking, "Why did he pick that one up?" He never praised. And he was very chauvinistic, actually. We've had our ups and downs, but I think he always believed in me as a teacher. And I think now he believes in me as an artist too. We have a very similar sense of abstraction. But he was brought up in a generation where women, by and large, weren't supposed to pursue a profession seriously. To a certain extent, we still battle that image, although it has its positive side. It helps in a woman's motivation to prove herself. That's part of the reason that I'm so strongly motivated. I want to be taken seriously, and that pushes me to work. I protect my ability to work above all else. To give you an idea of how far I'll go, I started doing hard-core exercises—push-ups, sit ups, five-pound weights—in order to carry my view camera.

JB: You once said that you came of age in a time when you lost your boyfriend if you wielded a camera, so photography had to be a private affair.

BC: That's right! Photography became my private world. I can be me when I'm photographing. I don't have to play any kind of role. My work means a lot to me for reasons that have nothing to do with pursuing art, and I wouldn't be surprised if that weren't the case for many artists.

Professionally, I've had to behave in a different way than a male photographer because there have been different standards of judgment. And I can't totally shake how I was brought up. I was brought up in a society wherein if a woman had too much education she'd never get a man. That was overtly spoken. So that now it's as if I'm a Jekyll and Hyde. I had to act sweet publicly, like women are supposed to act, or *were* supposed to act. I had to hide a lot of my motivation, as much as I *could* hide it. You want to be taken seriously, but what would be normal assertiveness for a man is considered aggressive for a woman.

I just want to add that I've done pretty well in the twenty years that I've been photographing in the art arena. I've amassed a large body of work for which I've gotten a lot of respect. My photography keeps me on an even keel, and I can bypass a lot of emotional problems and hurts by being involved in it. That's a lucky thing.

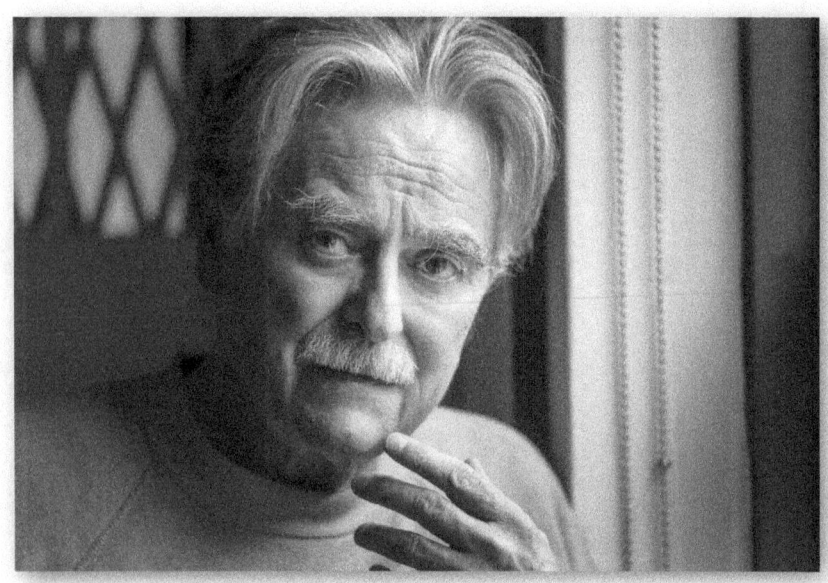

Photo by Eugene Pierce

Ticket to Danger

Published December 1984

In June 1983, *Time* photographer Bill Pierce and Associated Press photographer Bill Foley were stalking Yasir Arafat in Lebanon's embattled Bekaa Valley. They were stopped by Syrian troops who, convinced they were spies, bound their hands behind their backs and brutally beat their driver.

Four hours later, the Syrians were finally persuaded that Pierce and Foley weren't spies but photojournalists. They released their captives. By that time, Pierce's right hand and wrist had turned blue and swollen, having suffered extensive nerve damage from the crushing ropes. "I told God, a hand isn't much to pay if you'll just get me out of this alive," Pierce recalls.

As he does after every combat assignment, Pierce swore he would never again photograph in a war zone. But a few months later, his hand returned to normal, and he was back in Lebanon.

Pierce won the 1983 Overseas Press Club Award for his coverage of Beirut, Northern Ireland, and Cairo. His photographs are featured in *War Torn* and the bestseller *Children of War*. But he resents being called a war photographer, and he doesn't believe his photographs will have any effect on the ferocity or frequency of wars.

This Princeton alumnus and one-time student of W. Eugene Smith obviously does his job well. But why does he do it at all?

JB: You're best known for the photographs you've taken in war zones, but I've heard that you prefer not to think of yourself as a war photographer.

BP: That's right. I like to think of myself as a generalist concentrating on news photography. As a contract photographer for *Time,* I've photographed science, medicine, and environmental stories, and I do a percentage of *Time*'s entertainment and arts coverage—basically anything they ask me to do. I also do some portraiture and work for other magazines. I don't know any war photographers, *per se.* People who are identified as war photographers usually take offense to it.

JB: Do you?

BP: Most definitely. People idolize war photographers. It's flattering to be thought of as brave and heroic and to go to cocktail parties and hear people say, "Wow, you must be one *hell* of a guy." But the flattery is misguided. The real bravery is in documenting the things you care about even when it means sacrificing comfort and a peaceful home life and putting up with an abrasive professional life in which people find your images useful but really wish you'd get rid of your point of view. I photograph wars for the same reason I photograph other things— because they're important. But I certainly don't want to make a career of photographing war, and I am not by any stretch of the imagination a brave person. I've gotten caught in adventures that made me *look* brave, but *that* didn't take any courage. The courage is in going there. I'm scared to death when I'm going there.

JB: You mean on the plane, en route?

BP: Yes. On the plane, I'm scared to death. I calm down when things start happening. And you know it's not all action. The heroism is not in covering the spectacular, dangerous events but in getting up each day knowing things could turn dangerous at any moment and working under that pressure. That's what takes balls.

JB: What was your first experience photographing armed conflict?

BP: Covering the Civil Rights Movement here. That was the first time I ever got fired on—the first time anybody pointed a gun at me.

The first time I was imprisoned or tossed around by large people in uniforms was in Poland in 1969.

JB: Why were you imprisoned?

BP: I was in Gdansk when the original workers' strikes that preceded solidarity started. Lest you think I was a crusading war photographer, I was there doing a geography and social studies book. I took a picture of a bread line, and the officials who were escorting me told me, basically, "You can speak about your poverty and you take pictures of it. We think that's very foolish. Here, we do not allow you to take pictures of poverty. That is officially a bad photograph, and you are now under detention for interfering with the government." When they let me out, they told me to leave as quickly as I could, so I hopped on the first plane, which was into Prague. That was days before the Russians moved in. For a geography and social studies book, it was a hell of a trip.

JB: What was the first war you photographed?

BP: Northern Ireland in 1976. John Durniak, who was then the picture editor at *Time,* asked me to go to the South of France to do a story on low-calorie gourmet cooking. I got as far as England and telexed John from the London Bureau explaining that I was sure he'd be much happier if I were in Belfast doing real news. And John, being the gentleman he is, agreed. Actually, he was furious because he had to find somebody else to do low-calorie gourmet cooking in the South of France, which everybody knew was going to run. It was highly doubtful that any of my pictures of Northern Ireland would run. In fact, they didn't. But it was an incredible experience for me. I was frightened to death by things I wouldn't be frightened of anymore.

JB: What made you do it?

BP: I just felt it was terribly important—that something terribly wrong was happening there. And when I arrived, I found it *was* awful.

I saw an incredible denigration of human rights—in society, in the courts, in every respect. I felt that as a journalist, this was what I should be photographing. I still feel that way. I don't feel comfortable doing it, but I think it should be done, so I do it.

JB: What frightened you then that doesn't frighten you now?

BP: I'm no longer afraid of walking up to the periphery of a battle. That first time I was afraid because I wasn't yet familiar with weapon trajectory and things like that. I was deathly afraid of being wounded. Now, I know how far I can go before I'm in trouble.

JB: Why didn't *Time* use your photographs?

BP: It just wasn't that big as news events go, but when the hunger strikers came along, I packed the magazine. Then I did a lot of the photography—including the cover—for *Children of War*. Roger Rosenblatt, who wrote the original story, expanded the text into a book and turned me into one of its characters. A few of my photographs were illustrations.

JB: When you photograph a war, what kinds of pictures do you look for?

BP: I'm interested in taking pictures of people everywhere. Not just in wars. When I'm in a war, I take pictures of people and how they respond to the war, to being caught in its aftermath or to being trapped in a culture that's been shaped by conflict.

JB: Are there pictures you won't take?

BP: Personally, I don't have any desire to take pictures of shells exploding on the horizon or of soldiers firing guns—big or little. I hope I wouldn't take pictures that misrepresented somebody. I don't want to do cheap shots that make people look villainous or heroic when they're not. Then there are the ones where a soldier points a rifle at you and says, "Don't take that picture!" That's a big category!

JB: Does that happen often?

BP: It's very common. In some parts of the world, it's a daily occurrence.

JB: How do your subjects react to you when you're photographing? Are they glad you're there? Are they resentful? Do they feel that you're helping their situation by documenting it? Or do they completely ignore you?

BP: All of the above. There's no predicting what people's reaction will be. But in general, most people are understanding, sympathetic, and helpful. There have been one or two people who became extremely upset at my taking pictures and who tried to exercise violence on me. But isn't that understandable? Their reaction actually makes more sense to me than when people let me intrude on their lives at a time when leaving them in privacy would be a normal and natural courtesy. Perhaps these people think I'm helping. I hope I am. But I don't believe I am to the degree that they think I am. The one thing I hear constantly is, "Tell our story. If you tell our story, then everybody will support us, and the situation will change."

JB: Do you think your photographs can make a difference?

BP: No. That is a sadly naïve view. I don't think that my pictures have ever accomplished anything in and of themselves.

JB: Have you always felt that way? Or is this the voice of experience?

BP: It's definitely the latter. We go out thinking we're going to change the world. People will look at our pictures and say, "My God! This is horrible? We must beat our swords into ploughshares! We must put down our guns!" And of course they don't—our pictures don't make them do that. If anyone is changed, it's those of us who take the pictures. I don't think we start out as particularly brave or courageous or sensitive. But all the changes that we, as photojournalists, want to make in people by showing them pictures of the horrors of war happen to us. That's why I'm so proud of the people I work with in those situations. They're the finest people in the world. If the world was filled with people who were lucky enough to have the kinds of experiences we've had it'd be a much more peaceful world. No doubt about it.

JB: That kills my next question. I was going to ask if there's any truth to the old stereotype of photojournalists as ruthless and competitive.

BP: The majority of photojournalists are not competitive in those situations. In fact, they're very supportive of each other. They have to be. This is not a racket where you can work alone. But I know of one or two selfish, egocentric nutcases who are competitive in the bad sense—who purposely mislead other photographers or become so aggressive while they're photographing that they create trouble. They're insensitive not only to other photographers but to their subjects, and if they continue to photograph in areas where they're at risk, they're going to get killed because other photojournalists simply stop associating with them, and they lose the protection of companionship. They've come up to me, for example, and said, "Bill, can I ride with you?" And I've told them," No, you can't. In fact, I don't ever want you to ride with me, and I don't want to see you near me." If that sounds unusually brutal, it's because my ass is on the line.

JB: There's no doubt that yours is a dangerous profession. How close have you come to being killed?

BP: Pretty close. Almost everybody I know who's worked those assignments has come close to being killed. You go out, and you never know what's going to happen. You're caught in shelling, and if a shell lands one place, you're dead. I've had friends killed, and it wasn't because they were nutcases or cowboys. They were just unlucky. Their deaths are not only the loss of friends; they're a grim reminder of what might happen to you.

JB: Knowing that, why do you continue to put yourself in risky situations?

BP: At any given time, I'm not sure that I *will* continue to put myself in those situations. I *never, ever* have the intention of going back. Then something happens, and I'm more qualified than someone who might be unfamiliar with the area or who doesn't have contacts, or I'm bored, so I go.

JB: But there must be something exhilarating about being there that keeps you going back and keeps you going when you get there.

BP: Well, sure. When you first get into an area, it's almost like Boy Scout camp. There are all your friends whom you haven't seen for months, and if the area is really embattled, you're outdoors eating out of tin cans. You're marching around in a strange environment. And you feel good because you're doing something important. All that doesn't override the fear, but it certainly dims it.

JB: Let me ask you a few technical questions. Which cameras do you use on assignment?

BP: I use 35mm Leicas and mechanical Canon reflexes. I've been using the new Canon F1 because it gives me some of the electronic features like automation and extended slow shutter speeds but also provides a mechanical backup in case there's a battery failure. It's also built into a slightly more rugged casting, so it can take more abuse than some of the more feature-laden, totally electronic cameras. I'm experimenting with some of those because they're lighter and smaller, but they're supplementary cameras.

JB: How many cameras do you carry with you?

BP: On a normal sort of feature-type war where it's not really run-and-duck time, I'll carry three cameras and four lenses—a 28mm, a 50mm, a 135mm, and a 300mm. If it's run-and-duck time, I'll carry two cameras. I never bring less than six cameras—I leave backup bodies at the hotel—and that does not include the lighter, more automatic cameras that are supplements.

JB: I notice a number of black-and-white photographs on your wall. Are they yours?

BP: The ones shot with an 8 x 10? Yes they are.

JB: Obviously, you don't spend all your time behind an SLR.

BP: No, and in fact a significant number of photographers who make their living from the publication of tiny, postage-stamp-sized color pictures shoot larger format black-and-white. We do it to regain control of our medium—and not just photographic control, but emotional control too. Obviously, we can do things with larger format black-and-white that are visually very different from what we do with a motorized semiautomatic SLR stuffed with Kodachrome. But we also can approach photography more contemplatively, spending what would normally be an inordinate amount of time on a single image. It's both therapeutic and important to your craft. The common denominator of all people who have done well photographing violence is that they have also done very well photographing nonviolence. Often, they've done it in the same arena. Susan Meiselas, who is famous for her photographs of violence in Central America, has also done some exquisite photographs of peace in Central America. Or at least what passes for it. You're not going to be a good photographer in nasty situations if you're not a good photographer.

JB: Are you a self-taught photographer?

BP: I'm completely self-taught. As far as school goes, I always recommend to aspiring photographers that they attend a school that offers a broad range of subjects because for one thing those are the last few years they'll be allowed to concentrate on great—if not very productive—ideas. And obviously, you have to bring more to photojournalism than just the ability to take a picture. Anybody can go to a newspaper and say, "I was trained as a photojournalist." I would bet the editor's response would be, "Listen, sweetie. In the next six months *I'll* teach you photojournalism. What else can you give me? An insight into science? Politics?" I believe the *craft* of photography is best learned in an apprentice situation.

JB: You yourself apprenticed with W. Eugene Smith, didn't you?

BP: It would be better to say that I was an acquaintance to whom he was kind. Gene was a journalist. People didn't follow him around when he was shooting. I did proof prints and correspondence for him. And like everybody around Gene, I learned a hell of a lot. Mostly, he taught me ethics. And you couldn't be around Gene without learning a great deal of craftsmanship.

JB: When you say he taught you ethics, what do you mean?

BP: On the most simplistic level, he taught me that photographers are responsible for their subjects. Cameras don't necessarily tell the truth. You can make your subject look like a fool, or you can make him look better than he is. Gene taught me that if you're doing news, you make very, very sure your photographs represent what is happening to the best of your ability. And you treat your subject photographically with the same respect and dignity you treat him on human terms.

JB: Counting the years you worked with Smith and then for *Time,* you've been observing news coverage for almost two decades. How do you think photojournalism has changed in that time?

BP: I think that because of television, people have become very aware of the power of pictures. And every army, even the smallest militia, has somebody to create photo opportunities that will make their side look good. They want you to see how happy and well their soldiers are, so they'll allow you to photograph the troops receiving mail from home and things like that. Or they'll take you out to the ships and let you take pictures of the galleys preparing three thousand turkeys "for our boys." That kind of crap. And we do it. The flip side is they want to make damn sure you don't take any pictures that will make their side look bad. They'll always say it's for security reasons. "You can't take that because it would reveal our positions. You can't go there because it wouldn't be safe for you."

JB: So it's become a public relations game.

BP: That's exactly right, and when you talk PR, you're not talking about logic, you're talking about visceral, nonverbal communication, and that's photography. It's photography that says, "These are the good guys," and everyone knows it. Here's a good example. Not too long ago, Eddie Adams tried to take a picture of an Israeli soldier kicking a prisoner. Another soldier pushed Eddie's camera down and said, "You can't take that." Eddie said, "Why not?" The soldier told him, "We don't kick our prisoners."

Even the lowliest foot soldier has become visually consummate and hip. I was photographing in Beirut. We had moved down to the front lines and it was moderately nasty—there were still some shells falling. I came across an old woman screaming in the courtyard of a bombed-out building because her two grandchildren had just been killed. The bodies had already been moved out, but there were three little infant's sneakers scattered around the courtyard in pools of blood—I don't know what happened to the fourth sneaker. I started to photograph one of these sneakers in its pool of blood, and a soldier who was standing nearby stopped me. He went and picked up the other two sneakers, and then he brought them over to me and set them down next to the other so there were now three bloody sneakers in the pool of blood. He looked at me, and he said, "Now good. You take this. Better now. Right?

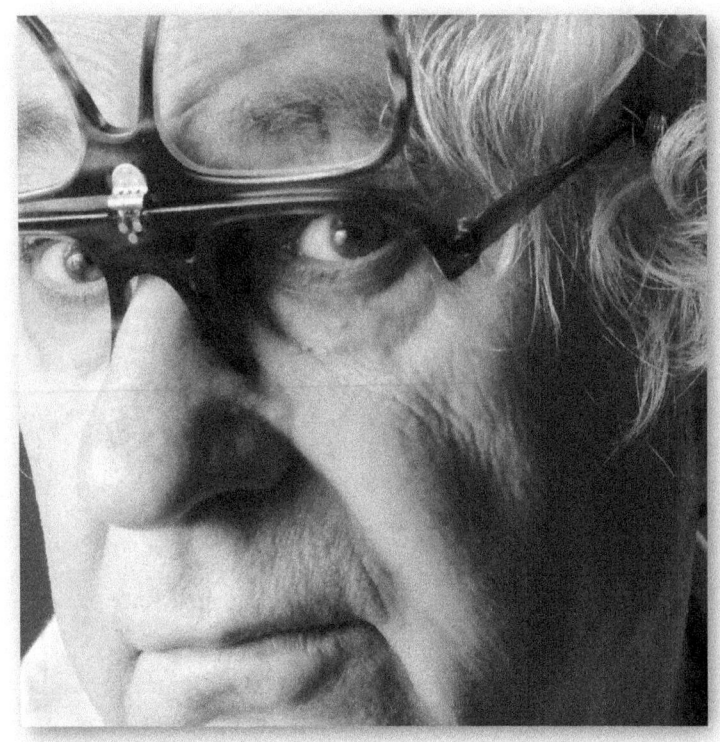

Photo by René de Carufel

ELLIOTT ERWITT (1928–)

A Wry Eye

Published January/February 1985

P hotography is Elliott Erwitt's business. It's also his hobby. For over thirty years, Erwitt has been a highly successful photojournalist, commercial photographer, and lately, filmmaker. In between—and sometimes during—assignments, he takes black-and-white snapshots that reveal, among other things, a healthy and complex sense of humor. His images have been collected in several books—*Photographs and Anti-Photographs Recent Developments* and the well-known *Son of Bitch*. He's gathering beach snaps for his next book. He threatens to call it *Son of Beach*.

Born in Paris in 1928, Erwitt moved with his family to Italy, back to Paris, and then to the United States, finally settling in Los Angeles. By the age of sixteen, he was a professional photographer. After moving to New York, he made the customary rounds, and with help from Roy Stryker, Edward Steichen, and others, found employment. Robert Capa took him into Magnum's fold in 1953. Later, as Magnum's president, Erwitt led the crusade for photographers to retain copyright to their work.

JB: Have you always distinguished between your personal and your commercial photography?

EE: Always. One is my hobby and the other is what I do for money. That's the only distinction. It doesn't mean that one is better or worse than the other or unworthy. It's just that I would not normally get up in the morning and say, "Well, today I think I'll go photograph a factory." However, if somebody pays me to do it, I will cheerfully get up and go photograph the factory. That's the distinction.

JB: Why do you do your personal work only in black-and-white?

EE: I just don't like color. It makes a great deal of sense to shoot motion pictures or commercial assignments in color because there you're after information. In my personal photography, I'm not interested in information. I'm interested in observation. You can abstract things in black-and-white in a way that you cannot in color. Frankly, black-and-white is far more difficult to do, although far simpler to look at. I believe that everything looks more or less okay in color. I don't know. Color seems…vulgar to me—sort of like Revlon ads.

JB: Many of your photographs are humorous. When you frame those shots, are you looking at something that's making you laugh?

EE: I don't know that I look for anything in particular. If some of my pictures are funny, I'm very pleased, because I'm interested in humor, but that's not my reason for taking the pictures. My photographs are nothing more than observation, and some of the things I observe happen to be amusing. When you have to put things together for a book or an exhibit, very often you have to come up with a theme. So okay. You've got dog pictures. I have no particular interest or disinterest in dogs, but I've got a lot of dog pictures. The same goes for humor. I suppose many of my pictures are humorous, but then many of them are not humorous. If I'm putting together an exhibit, I might group the humorous pictures because then there's a theme. But it's just packaging.

JB: Do you own a dog?

EE: Not at the moment, no. I haven't for a while. Dogs require more care than people. I've sort of been collecting children instead.

JB: And beach pictures.

EE: There are a couple of reasons for that. First, beaches are a good place for observing things that I'm interested in. Second, I like to go to the beach to relax and rest every so often, and I might as well do something useful while I'm resting.

JB: For me, one of your most memorable photographs is one that was taken at a nudist camp. A gentleman in the foreground is holding a few baseballs. He's looking across at a woman who's bending over. She has a birthmark on her rump that looks suspiciously like a bull's eye. How did you come to be taking pictures in a nudist camp?

EE: Well, everyone's got to be somewhere.

JB: Were you on assignment?

EE: Yeah, I was on assignment for the now vanished *Holiday* magazine. That was one of my very best stories. It was not published. I don't know why because the pictures are very, very innocent. But I had a wonderful time. I visited nudist colonies all over Europe.

JB: Did the nudists know they were being photographed?

EE: In most cases. People are nudists because presumably they're not ashamed of walking around without clothes. They're essentially exhibitionists. In fact, one of the most popular activities at nudist camps is taking pictures of one another. So they can't object very much to being photographed, providing they have some notion that you're not exploiting them or doing something tacky.

JB: A few of your photographs, like the "Kitchen Debate" between Nixon and Khrushchev and the shot of Jackie Onassis at JFK's funeral are so well known they've become emblematic of your work. They're certainly not representative. Do you resent that?

EE: I resent nothing. Why should I resent it if a picture becomes known? The only thing I resent about the "Kitchen Debate" picture—and it has nothing to do with the picture—is that the Nixon reelection campaign used it without my permission. I was annoyed about that because I certainly was not for Nixon. But I'm delighted with the picture. It's an amusing picture.

JB: Were you on assignment then?

EE: Yes, I was in the Soviet Union photographing at the American Fair. I was working for Westinghouse and, as I remember, I was taking pictures of their installation. But obviously when events happen you don't just put your camera away. Nixon and Khrushchev were touring the exhibits. They stopped at Macy's kitchen and got into a discussion. Since silly words were exchanged and since reporters were there, it became a media event called the "Kitchen Debate."

JB: There was an actual kitchen set up there?

EE: Yeah, it was like an industrial fair set up to show American wares to the unwashed Russians—to show them how advanced we were. That's what the debate was about, on the lowest possible level. But that was perfectly in keeping with the people debating it.

JB: What kind of camera did you start out using?

EE: A Leica. I mostly use Leicas.

JB: Did you study photography?

EE: Well, I have certain opinions about studying photography. I took a couple of photography courses, but that's hardly studying photography. You don't study photography. You do it. All you need to study is the instructions on the box of film. The rest is application.

JB: Did you come to that conclusion as a result of your own studies? Or from having seen the work of photo school grads?

EE: No, no. I don't mean to put down photography schools. They're a perfectly pleasant way to spend time—to meet people and exchange hypos or whatever people do there. I suppose some people feel they need structure or discipline, but you might as well go to a school for basket weaving. And in fact, I think basket weaving is probably more complex than photography in the sense of technique.

JB: When did you come to New York?

EE: I came to New York several times while I was still living in Los Angeles because I couldn't bear LA, at least to live there. I tried New York out a few times in the late forties and early fifties. I worked here just before I was drafted into the army in 1951. Since I got out in 1953, I've always lived here.

JB: How did you come to work with Roy Stryker at Standard Oil?

EE: I was making my rounds in the early fifties, as people do when they come to New York, and I went to see him with my pictures. I guess he liked what he saw, and I was an eager young fellow, so he tried me out. He was a very giving person. And perceptive. He thought I needed a job, which I did, so he hired me on the spot.

JB: Stryker seems to have had a profound effect on people who worked with him. Gordon Parks, for instance, says that Stryker was one of the most influential people in his life in terms of directing him and teaching him what to look for when he photographed. Did you learn the same sorts of things from Stryker?

EE: Absolutely not. Stryker was a nice, decent man. The substantial thing he did for me was give me a job. He also did other things that were not so attractive. He kept my negatives. Obviously, when you're seventeen or eighteen years old you don't think about those things, but in retrospect, I'm really quite annoyed that I lost my earliest work. I seem to have kept everything *but* that. But that's the way things were. It was difficult to know then that one's negatives might be useful in later life.

JB: Have you tried to get them back?

EE: Well, theoretically, I could borrow them if I knew where to locate them, but that's different from having them myself, and other people have access to them and can use them in any way they want. Of course, there should be no complaint because those were the rules. I believe, however, that it's wrong, and certainly the stuff should have reverted to the photographers after some time.

JB: You also met Steichen when you made your rounds, didn't you?

EE: Yes. I needed a job again, so he sent me to Valentino Sarra, who was a commercial photographer with a big studio. He was a really gross, bad photographer. He did the worst kind of photography that was being done then. You know, people with tennis rackets and Vaseline on their brows? However, it was a small factory of photography, and it was very, very instructive to work in such a place and see how the big boys did it then—and still do now in other styles. It was a great lesson.

JB: Were you a photographer's assistant?

EE: No, I was lower than that. You see, at that time if Steichen called somebody and said, "I've got a nice young fellow here, why don't you give him a job?" they'd give him a job whether they needed someone or not. So I was hired and after the favor was done—and it didn't take long—I was fired because they didn't really need me. But in the few weeks I was there I happened to notice a few very significant things. The most significant was that in commercial photography, the least important thing to know is photography. The most important thing to know is how to do business.

JB: How did you hook up with Magnum?

EE: One of the people I met during that period was Robert Capa. I looked him up in Paris when I was in the army, because that's where he was living. He was extraordinary, just as legend has it. He liked what he saw, and so he told me that when I got out of the army, he would take me into Magnum, which he did.

JB: The chroniclers of your career never fail to point out that you were eager to take on any assignment when you first started out because you wanted to establish a reputation for being willing to do anything. After a while, though, were there assignments you would turn down?

EE: Taking on any assignment was a kind of arrogance on my part. Certainly there are jobs I prefer to others, but you don't take jobs to fulfill your innermost needs. There are those occasional jobs that somehow fit in with your point of view and what you'd like to do, but that's unusual. Some photographers are able to kid themselves into thinking that what they're doing for their customers is their life's mission. That's fine for them, but that has never been the case for me. And I don't think that's a problem at all. I really don't believe you have to love what you do to do it well. I think if everybody loved what he did—although most people seem to say that they do—it would be a very sad day. Because look at all the crap that's around. How can you love that?

JB: Were you blackballed at *Life* magazine at one point?

EE: Many of us Magnum photographers were blackballed from Time Inc., the parent corporation, when we were fighting to hold onto our copyrights. Because Time Inc. was very powerful, it could make certain immoral demands on photographers. They required freelancers to turn over all rights if they wanted to work. Freelancers have to make a living and they're very susceptible to lack of work. I suppose that was one way of beating photographers into submission. But they didn't succeed in the end, and with that we set a precedent that's still adhered to today. There was really absolutely no reason, and there is still no reason, why anybody who commissions work should own it and make a profit out of it beyond the initial use.

JB: Are there any contemporary photographers whose work excites you?

EE: There are a *lot* of photographers whose work puts me to sleep. There are very, very few interesting photographers, in my opinion. There are armies of competent, slick, professional, tolerable photographers who don't pollute the atmosphere too much. One needs only to open magazines and look up on billboards to see their work. On the level of art, or what you will, there are very few. There are some, obviously. But that's how it should be.

JB: Like who?

EE: I'm not going to say. Why go through laundry lists? I would only say that photographers who have a point of view and who have something to say, who do not have predigested views and who do not mold their observations around a technique—whether it be a specific camera or a wide-angle lens—those are the people who are interesting.

JB: Do you have a favorite photograph?

EE: Of my own? Not particularly.

JB: Of anyone else's?

EE: Yes. I have a couple of pictures upstairs that I like a lot. I have a Lartigue, which is the most elegant picture I think I've ever seen. It's of a lady—it must have been one of his wives—reclining on a sofa looking beautiful. André Kertész once gave me one of his pictures, which is one of my favorites—Satiric Dancer.

JB: Do you have a darkroom here?

EE: Yeah, I have a very nice, private little darkroom that I rarely use anymore.

JB: Do you have assistants to do your printing?

EE: I would love to have an assistant who prints. It is harder to find a good printer than it is to find a good photographer. Anybody can make a print, but a printer who understands value and prints properly is just about as rare as the dodo bird.

JB: Are you working mainly on films now?

EE: The last couple of years have been mainly films. Now I want to get back to photography. Unfortunately, you can't suddenly decide, okay, this afternoon I'm going to go out and take some wonderful pictures. It has to evolve. You have to have an atmosphere. So I'm going to try to reserve some time for that.

JB: What films are you working on now?

EE: I've just finished two. I've been doing a series called "Great Pleasure Hunts" for Home Box Office. They're satirical films made all over the world. They have to do with excess. The one that's on the air now is called "Great Pleasure Hunt Part III." One of the themes is the ultimate meal. Actually, what we're exploring is which is better, food or sex? The resolution is that they're both pretty good.

JB: That sounds interesting.

EE: The last one, number four, is titled "The Great Pleasure Hunt USA." The theme, loosely, is the self-improvement craze. The message is, why bother? It's all done as a joke.

JB: Has your knowledge of still photography helped you with filmmaking?

EE: Any picture—whether it's a still picture, a moving picture, a drawing, a painting, or anything two dimensional—has to have structure, composition, dynamics, and balance. Then too, point of view crosses over. Otherwise, films are really totally different from photography.

JB: One last question. Why did you take up photography anyway?

EE: Well, one has to do something. There's no great cosmic reason. I suppose photography appealed to me because it was something I could do on my own. It wasn't a *real* job. I've always resisted real jobs.

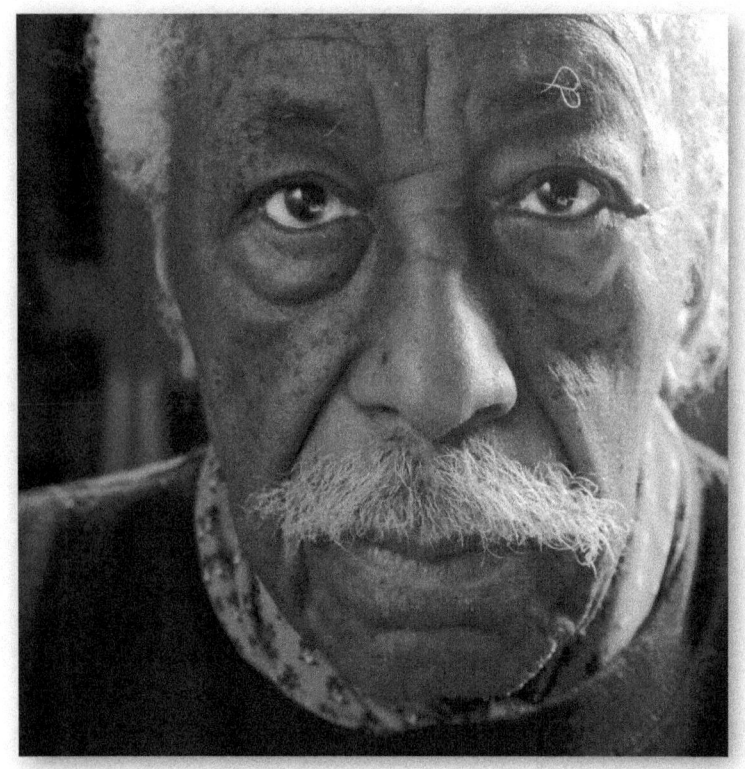

Photo by René de Carufel

GORDON PARKS (1912–2007)

Fighter with a Camera

Published March/April 1985

"**W**ho's going to be the most famous person in the room?" someone asked the mind reader who had been hired to entertain at the Rotary Club luncheon. "Gentlemen," he said, "There is a boy at the back of this room in a white uniform. He will be more widely known than anybody else here."

It was spring 1932. The mind reader was talking about a twenty-year-old busboy. His name was Gordon Parks.

Parks had a long way to go to live up to the mind reader's prediction, but live up to it he did. Born the son of a sharecropper in rural Kansas in 1912, the youngest of fifteen children, he spent his early years fighting hunger, poverty, and prejudice. From the age of sixteen, he was on his own, and after moving to St. Paul, he worked variously as a piano player, busboy, railway porter, and semiprofessional basketball player. Then he bought a camera.

In the second of three memoirs, *A Choice of Weapons*, Parks writes that one of the lessons of his childhood was that love, self-respect, and hard work are better ways to fight the world than hatred. These were the weapons he chose in his battle against poverty and injustice, and photography was another one.

Married and with a growing family, Parks moved to Chicago in his late twenties. While earning a living with fashion photography, he roamed Chicago's South Side, taking pictures he hoped would "strike at the heart of poverty." These photographs won him a Julius Rosenwald Fellowship, and he promptly joined the Farm Security Administration (FSA) photographers, a group that included Dorothea Lange and Walker Evans, in documenting the Depression.

Parks was the first black to join the FSA and later, in 1948, the staff of *Life* Magazine. A composer, poet, and filmmaker in addition to being a photographer and writer, Parks has authored a dozen books, including several novels, a book on photographic technique, and several volumes of poetry illustrated with his color photographs. He left *Life* in the late sixties to work on the film version of his novel *The Learning Tree*, a fictionalized account of his Kansas youth. He wrote the screenplay and musical score and produced and directed it, thus becoming the first black to direct a major motion picture. *Shaft* and *Leadbelly* are among his other directing credits.

Parks is now seventy-one. His East Side Manhattan apartment is proof of the rewards of hard work, even if the fact that he lives alone is proof of its hazards. In his spacious living room, floor to ceiling windows framed with greenery overlook the East River, and books are piled everywhere—on the antique writing table across the room, on the sofa next to us, on the cream-colored Oriental rug at our feet. Snapshots of his extended family (he married three times—four if you count a second marriage to his first wife) and friends crowd the top of a grand piano. His 30 x 40 color photographs hang on the walls.

It's Sunday, and after two weeks of daily phone calls, I've finally persuaded him to see me on his day of rest. He lists his reasons for being so evasive: He's just finished a film for American Playhouse. PBS is doing a special on his life, and they've been running him all over the country. There's a lecture to give here, a radio interview there. He's just beginning negotiations for a new motion picture, and he's working on a Broadway musical. His retrospective show is touring the country, and he attends the opening in each city. In and amid all of that, he says, he hopes to get off to a nice, beautiful island. Someplace. Anyplace. Just to rest.

I begin by asking him why he chose to become a photographer.

GP: I was in search of some way to express my feelings about my surroundings, about the things I liked and disliked, a way to voice my resentment, my feelings about poverty, discrimination, and bigotry. I felt that photography was the most organized, practical, and genuine way to do it. And it was quick.

JB: What was your first camera?

GP: A Voigtlander Brilliant. I thought the name was really right on. I got it in a pawnshop, and it cost five dollars and fifty cents. It wasn't much of a camera, but oh, what a name it had! The local Kodak store gave me a lot of encouragement after they developed my first roll. One of the clerks told me the results were excellent and asked how long I'd been shooting. I said it was my first roll. He told me that if I did two or three more rolls of film like that they'd give me a show. I couldn't believe the film even turned out because I thought I'd ruined it when I fell into Puget Sound trying to shoot some seagulls. I didn't even know how to unload the camera, so they unloaded it for me. Kodak *did* give me a show, about three or four months later—in the window of their downtown Minneapolis store.

JB: What were you doing to make a living then?

GP: I was running on the North Coast Limited between St. Paul, Chicago, and Seattle. At the same time, I was keeping my eyes open, learning to see things and mentally arranging visual compositions.

JB: Did you envision photography becoming a full-time professional career?

GP: I had to envision it as a career if I was going to pursue it because I just could not afford it as a hobby. I was too poor.

JB: How did you hook up with the Farm Security Administration?

GP: I'd seen the work of the FSA photographers—Dorothea Lange, Walker Evans, Arthur Rothstein, Russell Lee, Jack Delano—and I liked what they were doing. I had received a Rosenwald Fellowship, and the Rosenwald staff persuaded Roy Stryker, who headed the photographic division at the FSA, to take me on.

JB: You wrote in your third memoir, *To Smile in Autumn,* that Roy Stryker altered the course of your life more than any other person. How did he do that?

GP: By making me aware of the importance of the camera as a weapon against intolerance, injustice, and poverty, by teaching me simplicity of approach. At that time, there was tremendous prejudice and discrimination in Washington. The very day I arrived, Stryker took my camera away and said, "Go out into the city and buy a coke. Eat in restaurants. Go to movies." It was devastating. I found out a black person couldn't eat in the restaurants downtown. I couldn't go to the theaters. No one wanted to wait on me in the stores. I had foolishly thought Washington was the seat of democracy and that there I would find real freedom. Instead, I found mountains of prejudice. The worst in the country, possibly. Worse than in Mississippi or Georgia or Alabama.

I also learned very quickly that just to photograph a man who refused to sell me a ticket for the theater or who refused to feed me was not enough. Bigots look just like anyone else. There are very kind-looking bigots. I learned that I had to get at the roots of the evil by showing the things that caused it.

The very first picture I took there was the one of a black woman standing in front of an American flag with a mop in one hand and a broom in the other. It frightened the hell out of Stryker. When he saw it he said, "My God. You're going to get us all fired." In retrospect, I must admit it's not a subtle picture.

JB: While you were with the FSA, were you photographing mostly around Washington, DC?

GP: First, I was sent to New England—I suppose so I could get my feet wet. Roy figured I would have no problems there. And then I did quite a bit of stuff right there in Washington, DC. I was very enthused because I started working in the style of the FSA group. There will never be another opportunity like that for photographers. It was fabulous. I thought it would be a wonderful chance for me to use my camera in the ghettos around the country, but strangely enough, Stryker kept me out of the ghettos.

JB: Did you ask him to send you there?

GP: No. I was very content to do what he wanted me to do. I realized that I was in a training period. Many magazines wanted to do stories on me because I was the first black photographer in the FSA. But he wouldn't allow that because he thought I wasn't ready for the experience. I had moments when I thought, "Is he holding me back?" But I needed publicity like I need a hole in the head. I really hadn't learned anything yet. He was right. Stryker was a strange guy.

JB: How so?

GP: He was somewhat disliked by some people who felt he held too close a rein on them. Stryker liked to test your courage. He would let you get yourself right in the middle of something, and then he'd step away and let you work it out. You know, I was one of the few people he allowed to photograph him. He'd sort of hint that there was a photograph of him needed, and would I be interested in taking it? I never really knew why he selected me.

Basically, we all loved Roy. He was very supportive when I started to do more fashion photography. Some of the guys—documentary types—would say, "How can you do this?" Roy said to me, "Well, Jesus. There's nothing wrong with photographing a beautiful woman in a beautiful dress. And furthermore, your ability to do that might very well keep you from starving one day. So pursue it. Don't pay any attention to these guys." And he was right again. It paid off.

JB: In *A Choice of Weapons,* you suggest that politics and racism played a part in dissolving the FSA.

GP: It was during the Great Depression in the thirties, a time when Americans were starving and many families rode the highways in jalopies looking for work. Farmers were losing their land to the drought and dust storms. In revealing all this, the FSA project was in a sense an indictment of America. It could only have existed under a president like Franklin D. Roosevelt. Some Southern congressmen finally put enough pressure on him to convince him that money was being wasted for something that was purely an indictment of his constituency.

JB: Where did you go when the FSA dissolved?

GP: To the Office of War Information, where I became a war correspondent. I was assigned to cover the 332nd—the first all-black fighter-pilot group—as it escorted bombers over their targets in Europe. I was pulled from the assignment at the port of embarkation because, again, there were certain Southern pressure groups that didn't want black plots getting publicity. When that fell through, I went back to New York and hooked up again with Stryker, who was by then at Standard Oil in New Jersey.

JB: Shortly thereafter, didn't you experience one of Stryker's tests of courage?

GP: That's right. He encouraged me to buy a house, and then he laid me off for a few months without warning. So I wrote a book about photography. Franklin Watts published it.

JB: How did you start working for *Life*?

GP: I'd done a story for a magazine that had just gone out of business, so I went over to *Life* and showed the photos to the picture editor, Wilson Hicks. He called in John Dille, the human affairs editor, and Sally Kirkland, the fashion editor. Both of them egged Wilson to take me on, but Wilson was reluctant. He asked me what I wanted to do and off the top of my head, for no reason that I can remember, I said

I wanted to do something on the Harlem gangs. He said, "No. We tried that last year and got sued because one of the boys in the gang turned out to be a preacher's son." In other words, the story was faked. I said, "I can do it. I'm not going to fake it." So he offered me $200 to do the whole story. I thought that was insane. I'm sure he did too. He thought it would discourage me. But John Dille kept encouraging me to take it, so I did. He got me outside, and he said, "You know, you're on an unlimited expense account." That catapulted me immediately to the highest paid photographer on *Life*'s staff.

JB: How did you get the story?

GP: I went to see a detective friend up in Harlem. He told me that no gang leader with any sense would even *think* about letting me hang out with him for three months. Well, in walked Red Jackson. He gave the desk sergeant a good cursing out. I wondered why this sixteen-year-old kid wasn't getting his head bashed in. The detective told me it was because he was one of the toughest kids in Harlem. He ran a gang, and if I could get with him, my problems would be solved.

So I asked Red about it. I told him I was a *Life* photographer. He wanted to know what *Life* was. I asked him if I could hang out with him and photograph him. No, of course not. I said, well, could I drive you home? Nope. But after he saw my beautiful Buick sitting outside the precinct house, he changed his mind. On the way home, he sensed the luxury of having a chauffeur for a while, so he went to his gang and convinced them to let me photograph them.

A couple of the kids were killed while I was doing the story. It was a very important story to me. I realized how young men like Red, who have a certain talent for leadership but lack direction, could end up in prison or the electric chair. They just didn't have a chance.

I saw Red recently, believe it or not. I was walking through the Forty-Second Street subway when this rather roly-poly man walks up to me. He says, "Hey there, Mr. Parks. Do you know me?"

I said, "Red Jackson." I asked him what he was doing.

"I'm hustling." He was dressed very well, his shoes shined, looking kind of slick.

I said, "Got any kids?"

"Oh yeah, I got three kids."

And I said, "Well, are you married?"

He said, "No, I never got married. I had my kids by three different women. I never fell for that marriage stuff. But I take care of my kids. They all go to school. They're all good kids and I like 'em."

So I said, "Red, I'd like to see you sometime."

He said, "Yeah, yeah, yeah. I'd like to talk to you."

I never heard from him, but I'm sure I'll run into him once again— hustling somewhere.

JB: Right after you did that story, didn't *Life* send you to Paris?

GP: Yeah, with Sally Kirkland, to do the French collections.

JB: This was a very different world from the one you'd been brought up in. Did it seem unreal to you?

GP: It *was* unreal. Here I was going to Paris first class on the Queen Mary and dressing for dinner every night. In Paris, I was photograph-ing models who were *very* famous. I was living at the Hotel Crillon on the Place de la Concorde, being chauffeured in limousines going to the houses of Dior, Balenciaga, Balmain, Givenchy. I had a hell of a good time. I learned a lot, and I tried not to let it overwhelm me.

JB: During that first trip to Paris, *Life* asked you to join its staff.

GP: Yes, and before long I was assigned to the Paris bureau, which was a plum because usually you had to work on staff six, seven, eight years to even be considered for it. Why they sent me immediately, I don't know. I'm inclined to feel that they reasoned that with my fashion experience I could cover the collections and with my documentary background I could cover the communist riots that were happening all over Europe then. I was black. Perhaps they thought I would do better in Paris than I would in America. I stayed there about two years.

JB: When you did photo essays for *Life*, like those on impoverished families, how much time did you spend with your subjects before you started photographing?

GP: Just enough time to get them to feel that I was a friend and wasn't there to exploit them—that I wanted to expose their plight through photography. Occasionally, I felt like I was playing God. Sometimes it worked out, sometimes it didn't.

The Flavio story turned out well. That was a documentary of a Brazilian child who was dying from a respiratory disease. I eventually brought him to the United States, and he was cured at the Asthma Clinic in Denver. He owns his own home now, and he's doing very well. The Fontanelle story? Disaster. Absolute disaster. I wanted to show a typically poor Harlem family. After the story came out, readers sent in contributions, and *Life* got them a house out on Long Island. It burned down. The father and one son died in the fire. One of the daughters died three years later. Three of the boys are in jail on dope charges. Mrs. Fontenelle is back in Harlem. I went up to see her on Christmas Eve, to take her some money, and sat with her for about two hours, feeling that I was a part of her misfortune.

JB: Does she blame you?

GP: No, she feels that I did what I could—which I did. It's nobody's fault the old man came home drunk and went to sleep on the couch with a lighted cigarette. It didn't matter if it was Harlem or Long Island. The key to the whole unfortunate episode was a bottle of whiskey and a cigarette.

JB: Do you often find yourself getting close to the people you photograph?

GP: Oh yes. Very close. Too close. I get concerned with the kids and what they're doing. How they progress. I keep in touch as much as I can.

JB: Did you get to know Malcolm X as a consequence of photographing him?

GP: Yes. We were very close friends by the end of his life. I'm his daughter's godfather. Malcolm was very important to me. I learned a lot from him, and he claims he learned some things from me. One night, we were on a plane coming in from Chicago during the heat of the civil rights battle. He was sleepy. He laid his head on my shoulder and said, "Well, maybe *A Choice of Weapons* is the way. Maybe your book is what it's all about." Then he went to sleep.

JB: That must have been a very loaded time for you emotionally—covering the Civil Rights Movement. Was that a test of your objectivity?

GP: I *had* to remain objective. I couldn't hoodwink a big organization like *Life* with all its checks and double-checks, and I didn't want to. I wanted to be an honest reporter. I couldn't hoodwink Malcolm or Cleaver or any of those guys. They were all rather brilliant young men. I did, however, have to lay the law down. I said, "I don't want to see anything that you don't want me to report." I had to protect myself at *Life* by writing my own stories and checking them out. Checking the checker out too. He could call a simple protest meeting a mob and I could be in trouble. I had to walk a tight line, knowing that I could always back up any situation through honest reporting. "This is what you did. This is what I wrote. I'm not telling it out of school."

JB: Even so, I imagine you caught a lot of criticism from certain segments of the black community—much as Milton Coleman did recently for reporting Jesse Jackson's remark about "hymies."

GP: That's true. There was a time when I was afraid for my life because of a story I wrote on Malcolm X's death. But if you call yourself a reporter, you have to *act* like a reporter. Actually, Jackson shouldn't have said what he said and he can only blame himself—and he does. A leader must rise above that sort of thing and really accept all people with a true sense of brotherhood. That's possibly the most important thing I've learned during my lifetime.

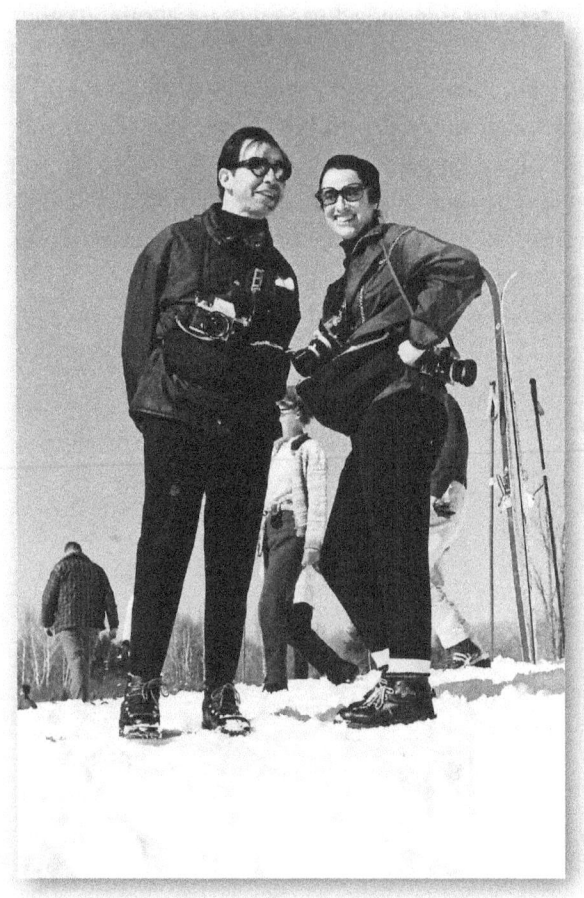

Photo by Robert F. George

SONJA BULLATY (1923–2000) AND ANGELO LOMEO (1921–)

Double Visions

Published September 1985

"**W**atch this!" Gears whir. A horn brays. The convertible comes to a stop. With a mechanical jerk, the woman on the passenger side gets up out of her seat and lifts a camera to her eye. A flashbulb pops, the woman is seated, and with a whir and a bray, the convertible resumes its journey across the hardwood floor. Laughing, Sonja Bullaty scoops it up and returns it to its place on the living room bookcase.

Sonja Bullaty and Angelo Lomeo are showing me their collection of photographica, a mixed bag of bright wind-up toys and rare antique cameras ranging from the sophisticated to those they describe as PHD cameras. "You know," says Bullaty, "Push Here Dummy?" The convertible is the collection's appropriate centerpiece—an obvious metaphor for the intertwined careers of Bullaty and Lomeo, wife and husband, both photographers.

Since 1947, three years before their marriage, they have traveled the United States and Europe together, pursuing assignments for *Life, Horizon, Audubon,* Champion, and Exxon, or documenting subjects of their own choosing. Based from their Manhattan apartment overlooking Central Park West, they've photographed people and places, cities and countrysides, fauna and flora. This latter includes so many New England autumns that they've taken to calling the landscape's plumage "foilage."

Bullaty and Lomeo work as a team and often submit their photographs with a dual byline, but the rule isn't hard and fast, and their viewpoints are distinct. They share a desire to communicate the beauty and fragility of the environment, but they both admit to having separate visual obsessions—Bullaty for the Kafkaesque shadows she remembers from her childhood in Prague and Lomeo for a witty appreciation of man's coexistence with nature.

Bullaty's father, a prosperous Jewish banker, gave her her first camera when Hitler invaded Czechoslovakia, and she was forced to leave school. She was fourteen. She spent the rest of her teens in concentration camps, where the remainder of her family died. Of those years and their effect on her photography, Bullaty, a tiny wisp of a woman with a ready smile, says, "When you have seen the depths of horror, you are so much more responsive to enormous joy. I celebrate life and beauty precisely because I have seen so much pain and ugliness."

Lomeo, in turn, grew up in an Italian-speaking family in Manhattan's tough Hell's Kitchen neighborhood. He studied painting and design at New York City's School of Industrial Arts before World War II interrupted. He served overseas, and then worked as a lumberjack in Montana, selling scenic photographs to tourists as a sideline. In 1946, Lomeo returned to New York City, determined to transform the sideline into a profession, at about the same time that Bullaty arrived from Europe.

JB: How did you meet?

SB: In the darkroom. Very apropos for your magazine, isn't it?

AL: I was managing a five-story studio on St. Marks Place—an entire building of darkrooms and studios that we rented to photographers. There was an open intercom on every floor, so everybody could hear what was going on. And I heard this charming voice on the intercom that I hadn't heard before.

SB: [Laughing.] He wondered about my accent.

AL: I went downstairs to investigate, and I saw Sonja in the darkroom.

SB: Scrubbing the floor.

AL: There she was, down on all fours.

SB: Believe me, I was very disgusted with a building run only by men.

AL: I hadn't seen anything like that since World War II. She must have had an inclination that somebody was there, because she suddenly turned around and was sort of embarrassed that I was watching her. I said, "You don't have to do that. We have people to take care of that sort of thing.'"

SB: Taking care all right. You should have *seen* how filthy it was.

AL: She said, "Who are you?" and I introduced myself.

JB: When did you start photographing together?

SB: About a year after that. We thought it might be a good idea to travel together and pool resources. Eventually, we decided it was kind of nice to *be* together so we got married in 1951, and we're *still* together. Amazingly.

AL: I'm amazed that you can remember what year it was.

JB: Photography is generally perceived as an individual's pursuit. After all, a viewfinder can only accommodate one eye. Yet you two often publish photos with a dual credit.

AL: Yes, but we have a lot with our own credits too. When we exhibit, our prints are signed individually—and exhibits are a major part of our life. And even though we work as a team on some projects, we each have our own distinct way of seeing. That's why we get such good coverage on assignments.

SB: Even when we're on the same location, we'll usually be back-to-back.

AL: Or we'll be literally side by side, looking at the same thing, but when we photograph it, we each come up with something completely different.

JB: When do you use the double credit, then?

SB: When we do a story or an assignment or a book together. For example, in our book *Circle of Seasons,* it doesn't say who took what picture, because we feel that what's important is the essay. If somebody's really curious, we've listed who took what in the back of the book. It's just that we're not on some insane ego trip. There's so much competition in the world, it's kind of nice to have a little bit of cooperation at home.

AL: I think we work together much better than if we worked alone. First of all, we carry our own equipment, so we can interchange it.

SB: I usually work with only two lenses, but it's very nice to be able to steal others from Angelo.

JB: You take on a variety of assignments now, mostly for book and magazine publishers. What kinds of things did you start out photographing?

AL: When we started working together, we established a reputation in the art world for photographing objets d'art—sculpture, painting, and furniture—mostly for art galleries and museums.

We worked with an 11 x 14 camera, which was fantastic training, both in good photography and good art. You decide that your work ought to measure up somehow to the wonderful objects you're photographing.

JB: Are you both essentially self-taught?

SB: Very much so. I worked with Josef Sudek in Prague for a while, but I just carried his equipment. I didn't really know what he was doing with those big boxes, except that he was trying to create magic. And he worked without an exposure meter. It was all pretty much in his head. I spent one year working with Sudek after the war and then came here in 1947.

JB: How did you get started in the United States as a professional photographer?

SB: I was extremely lucky. I found work with a photographer on my third day here. This man advertised for a tall, strong young man. I figured I had nothing whatsoever to lose, so I may as well introduce myself to him. I told him, "Look. I am strong, but I am not tall. I can always take a step stool with me."

AL: You told him, "I can do anything a man can do."

SB: Well, very definitely. "But," I said, "I am sorry, I cannot become a boy." That photographer was the exact opposite of Sudek because he was very scientific. He measured all his exposures and drove me absolutely insane because I couldn't figure out his mathematical formulas.

AL: That's about the time I met her. I had returned from World War II. I got a job as a wedding photographer, operating out of that building on St. Marks. I soon realized I didn't like that kind of work at all. At my suggestion, my boss put me in charge of running the building, doing the booking and sending the photographers out on their various assignments. In a way, it was a lot more work than just going out and shooting the weddings. Then I met Sonja, and we started photographing with the 11 x 14.

SB: Making 11 x 14 contact prints. Our printer is a homemade monstrosity that is better than anything made commercially. It's really quite marvelous.

AL: When they saw those prints, people really went crazy for them. We got a reputation for being able to shoot anything from 35mm to 11 x 14.

SB: Which we still do, but mostly we use 35mm.

AL: That view camera really developed a discipline in us. You have to get perfection on that ground glass.

SB: It was fantastic training. But life's so short, and when you work with a large camera, somehow life runs away. You get good but very static pictures. I feel very strongly that it's important to get some life into a photograph—a blur of wind or something like that. And we like to photograph animals in the wilderness. I would like to see somebody setting up an 11 x 14 camera and waiting for a bear.

AL: We just finished two children's books for Western Publishers using photographs of wild animals.

SB: It was something new—not that cutesy-pie sort of nonsense. You know, not the bears and the porridge, all staged, but the bears in real life. It came about because we did a book for Time-Life on the Southern Appalachians, and while we were photographing flowers and mountains, we came upon a full-grown male bear in a tree. So we photographed him. When we came back with the pictures, they sent us right back to do an essay on the life of the bears.

AL: So we went back. It took us two days, but finally we came across a mother bear and two cubs.

SB: The mother attacked Angelo.

AL: I was lucky that an expert on bears from the University of Tennessee was with us. He knew how to stop a bear if it comes at you. All you do is pick up a pebble. He went like that [makes a tossing motion], and the bear was startled by it.

SB: Screaming helps too. I really screamed.

AL: There was no way I was going to get away from that bear if he hadn't stopped her.

JB: How far away were you shooting?

SB: About ten feet.

AL: Which was stupid of me. I got into this trouble because at Time-Life they said, "Make sure you get a mug shot." You know? "Get close." I could have done that with a long lens, but I had either a 105mm or the 55mm on a motorized camera.

SB: About a year after we did that assignment for Time-Life, it was published in *Audubon,* and then we realized the photographs would make a great story for children, so we submitted the idea to Western.

AL: They printed it on very cheap stock, but despite that, they've sold 150,000 already. It's in the third printing. They told us that the people who buy these books don't look at the quality of the printing. Instead, they look at how a child will respond to the idea.

JB: I take it that you rough it when you tackle these projects.

SB: Yes, we backpack. We camp. In 1951, we took our first trip in a van.

AL: We were the original hippies. There were very few on the road then.

SB: It wasn't really a van. We took a half-ton Chevy truck and equipped it with a bed and camping and cooking equipment. We wanted to make it to the coast, but we ran out of money.

JB: Do you stick to the back roads?

SB: Oh yes! Have you read *Blue Highways?*

AL: We've been doing that for years—traveling on those blue roads.

SB: Reading that book was like being there again.

AL: We took a trip down south once. We were in Kentucky in the Appalachians, and we were going over these switchbacks, up one mountain, down another. We had looked at the map, and we thought that it would be interesting to take a back road through hillbilly country. And when we were really deep in it, we came across this guy standing in the middle of the road with a shotgun. He stopped us. Then he walked over to the side of the car, and he said, "Where y'all going?" I said, "I saw this road on the map, and I'm trying to get to the other side of this mountain." He said, "You ain't goin' nowhere. You gonna turn right around. And if you don't..." I said, "I get the message!"

SB: Someone told us later that we were probably right on top of his still.

JB: These trips are often self-assignments, aren't they?

SB: Oh yes. We still do that very often.

AL: My advice to all photographers is this: If you feel strongly about an idea, don't wait until you get an assignment. If you can afford it, go out and shoot it.

SB: Afford it or not afford it. If you take photography seriously, then sometimes the very best work that you do is your own idea.

AL: And these self-assignments, if they don't sell right away, they'll sell later. Ours have always sold.

JB: You've gone on the road on assignment quite often too. Tell me about some of your favorite assignments.

SB: We did a couple of assignments in Scotland for *Horizon* magazine years ago. The first one was based on Boswell's *Journey to the Hebrides*. We actually used that incredible book that was written in 1773 as a guide. We wanted to re-create its mood.

AL: That was fun.

SB: It was marvelous. *Horizon* published it beautifully, and they liked it so well that the next year they sent us to photograph Edinburgh.

AL: And over a period of time, every one of *Horizon*'s editors ended up taking their vacations in Scotland. That's when you know that a photo essay has succeeded. One of the pictures from Scotland was used on the cover of *Popular Photography.* You'd be surprised at the reaction we got because it's not the kind of photograph you usually see on their cover. People wrote to find out how they could buy the picture.

SB: We sold three prints as a result.

JB: It looks and sounds like you have a very congenial collaboration. But aren't there times when the two of you don't get along? When you can't agree on f/stops or something?

SB: You bet.

AL: Sure. Plenty of times.

SB: Of course, if we didn't fight like cats and dogs, we wouldn't be together anymore.

AL: Every now and then, a little fight is okay. But we usually work it out.

SB: Well…seriously, we do have a very specific problem. We not only live together, but we work together, so if we argue and it's of a personal nature, it'll carry over into our professional life and vice versa. There are times when we don't really like to talk to each other.

JB: I suppose it's only natural that you'd have differences—what about equipment? Do you favor different lenses and so on?

AL: We each have Nikon bodies but different lenses, so when we work together, we have quite a nice variety of lenses to use.

SB: I love my 28mm. That's really my overall working lens. And then I work with an 80–200mm zoom.

AL: I have a 55mm, an 18mm, and a solid optics 200mm that converts to a 400mm.

SB: And you have the 105mm.

AB: With those lenses, I can cover anything. I keep a 500mm in the trunk and some of the other big lenses that we use once in a blue moon. But once in a blue moon it pays off.

SB: Actually, we used them quite a bit in the Blue Ridge this past fall because the sunrises over there are just fantastic. Really special.

JB: What a life! How often are you out on the road?

SB: We travel quite a bit. And we have a place in Vermont, but we are not there nearly often enough!

AL: Luckily, we sell a few pictures each year to advertising, and that's what keeps us going.

SB: Pictures we've already done, and that's great!

AL: We get four checks a year from the Image Bank.

SB: People see things in books, and they sell. Thank God for that, because we don't go out very much to show our work. Well, let's face it. As salespeople, we are such gigantic failures that we might as well leave it to others.

AL: There are some photographers who are terrific salesmen. They can sell the lousiest pictures you ever saw and make the guy think he's got something great. We're the opposite. We show our pictures and convince the guy they're no good.

JB: Are you planning any special trips in the future?

AL: Sonja especially wants to go out West, to Death Valley. I want to go too, because if I don't get out West every now and then, I don't function very well. I spent my very young years as a lumberjack in Montana. So one of these days, we'll just pack up and go out there, and she'll do her thing, and I'll do mine, and we may come back with some strong new material.

SB: And usually, you know, it takes a few years before a trip like that is financially covered—the part that's not on assignment. But so what!

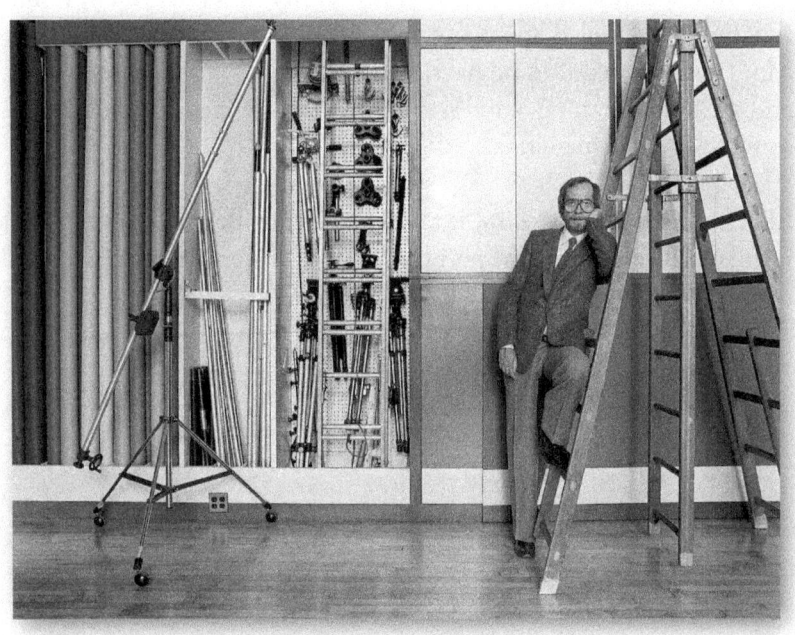

Photo by Kurt Fishback

The Turner Touch

Published December 1985

"That blue is my favorite color," says Pete Turner, referring to my royal blue sweater. This isn't news. My sweater happens to match the blue director's chair on which he's sitting, the fixtures in the bathroom, and many of the other furnishings in his compact Carnegie Hall studio. I mention that green is my favorite color, but few people look good in green. "Cole Weston looks good in green," says Turner, and launches into an anecdote involving a recent Weston trip to New York, a Japanese restaurant, and quantities of sake—colorful talk from Pete Turner, master color photographer.

Turner's long and happy career has been blessed not only by his prodigious talent and love of high-tech but with his knack for being in the right place at the right time. As a member of RIT's class of '56, he was one of the first to graduate from an accredited university course in photography. He joined the army in 1957, and was assigned to the pictorial service division, where he headed an experimental Type C lab. A perquisite of his army duty was the lush—and uncommon—color portfolio with which he later wooed magazine editors. He worked for *Horizon, Esquire, Look, Life*—all the big ones—before opening a commercial studio in 1966, just as the magazines started foundering. Since then, Turner has created his vivid Kodachrome fantasies and cool, graphic science fictions for the likes of Citicorp (the City of Tomorrow campaign) and Steven Spielberg (the famous *Close Encounters* poster). Testimony to another special Turner touch is the exceptional number of his assistants who've moved on to highly respectable careers of their own, among them Eric

Meola, Anthony Edgeworth, Michel Tcherevkoff, Ted Kaufman, and Steve Krongard. In certain circles, the Turner studio is known as Pete Turner U.

Our interview takes place on the narrow, blue-upholstered balcony overlooking the studio, attainable by a perilously steep spiral staircase. Below, Turner's studio manager confers with a duo of business-suited clients, while a second assistant mans the duping machine, and a third fields phone calls. Above, we talk.

JB: You're almost as famous for your assistants—many of whom have become top commercial photographers in their own right—as for your own photography. What's your secret?

PT: My assistants hire their own replacements. As the photographer, I feel I'm not really aware of the vibes with the staff—who gets along with whom. I try not to interfere with their decisions unless I sense someone's really not right for the studio. Michel Tcherevkoff was the first studio manager here. He hired Eric Meola.

JB: And the rest is history. Have you ever hired anyone over their objections?

PT: Only once. That was the case of Anthony Edgeworth. The assistants thought he was too old. He was in his midthirties and had been with Ralph Lauren in the clothing business, as well as involved in a few other nonphotographic pursuits. He had absolutely no experience. But I *saw* something in Anthony. He really wanted to be a photographer. I figured anybody that age who wanted to do something that badly should have the chance. We hired him, and he worked out wonderfully. He turned out to be a very good shooter. Just excellent.

JB: Most of your assistants, Edgeworth excluded, have been photography school graduates—as you are. Is that a requirement?

PT: Not really. I think schools are great. But John Harcourt, who runs the studio now, is self-taught. [Turner leans forward conspiratorially.] They're down there right now talking about scanners and million-dollar pieces of equipment that can do everything—probably drive you around the block. These are things I know nothing about.

JB: How many people work here?

PT: Three—Phyllis Giarnese, Rob Atkins, and John. Phyllis does production and runs the business side of the studio. She runs interference. Rob runs our duping program full time. Our dupes are made in multiples of between forty and seventy-five per image and disseminated worldwide through the Image Bank. We use a Marron Carrel printer. You just punch in the number of chromes and the machine does all the work for you. It beats the old duping system of one at a time. And when we get big jobs, we hire freelance assistants.

JB: Is commercial photography as lucrative and glamorous as it's made out to be?

PT: Well, I think it *was* very lucrative. It's extremely competitive right now and the mass-market magazines, which were my entrée to commercial photography, have dribbled down to nothing. In the old days, if you published in *Look, Life, Holiday,* or *Esquire,* almost every art director saw your photos and looked at them very carefully. Now, there are all these special interest magazines like *Popular Boating, Popular Golf,* popular this, popular that. So if a photographer shoots a boating story, it goes into *Popular Boating,* and only those enthusiasts will see it. In the old days, it went into *Sports Illustrated,* and everybody saw it. But it's fun to be involved in photography today, or film, or writing. When you look at the world and some of the jobs people have to do, you appreciate having work like this.

JB: If you can make a living at it—which you've obviously managed to do. Is specializing in color part of your secret?

PT: Well, I didn't get interested in color because I thought I'd make more money at it. I've just always loved color. But there's no doubt that I have a good standard of living. I have a nice studio. I have a condominium here in the city and a house and property out in East Hampton. I'm not on welfare. But acquisitions were never too much of a thing with me. I just need to be able to get away for a weekend out in the country. I just need a nice fireplace and some nice sticks around me.

JB: Your career seems to have been charmed from the start.

PT: It wasn't all *that* easy. There were very few magazines that counted, and boy, if you wanted to work for them, you had to be established. My big break came after I'd been out of the army for five or six months. I hooked up with the Freelance Photographer's Guild, and one day a fellow came to the office looking for someone to spend six months in Africa. Did I want to go? I said, "Yippee!" The guy was with Airstream Trailers, and they wanted me to photograph a promotional trek through Africa. They set me up with an RV that had everything in it. It could go over anything.

I came back with photographs of Africa, and I also had images I'd made while I was in the army, when I ran a Type C lab. In fact, it was my duty in the army to go out and take pictures and make color prints. So I had a big portfolio of C prints and pictures of Africa.

I made the rounds with the portfolio, which was unusual because of the amount of color, and met Harold Hayes, then the editor of *Esquire*. He took to me. He was a great editor because he knew how to direct a photographer. And he was a wonderful mentor. He'd say, 'I'd like you to shoot John Dos Passos." And I'd say, "John who?" Harold would just laugh. He'd say, "Well, he's an interesting guy. He's written a few books."

JB: You were doing a lot of editorial work in the sixties. Then you switched to commercial illustration. Was that an abrupt change or something that came about gradually because of the market?

PT: It happened in 1966.

JB: That sounds fairly abrupt.

PT: I'd one an entire issue on Scandinavia for *Holiday*. When I came back, I learned they had both new editors and a new art director. No one had bothered to tell me while I was away. I was absolutely shocked. It seemed so unprofessional. Here I was doing an entire issue of their magazine, and no one took the time to telex me about these changes. I came back with the pictures, and they ended up using what I considered to be outtakes—almost the opposite of what I'd been aiming for. It was pretty depressing at the time.

Then, looking around, I realized a lot of magazines were having problems. I decided since I'd been making reasonably good money through advertising anyway, why not open a studio? That's exactly what we did.

JB: But you do still take on editorial assignments.

PT: Yes. If there's something I really want to photograph, I'll get myself an assignment, although I really lose money on editorial work. I have to maintain my staff here, and then I go off to, say, Australia, into the outback. With jet lag and editing time and everything else, you're talking three to four weeks. But it lets me get out there and make my own images. Ultimately, I do make some money by distributing them through the Image Bank. I went to India and Africa for *Geo*. Most recently, I did a story on the Pinnacle Desert in Australia for *Science Digest*. I work for *Omni*. Those are the fun things. But basically, our overhead advertising covers our overhead.

JB: Do you ever turn down commercial assignments?

PT: Not very often. But if they're really not my cup of tea, I recommend somebody else because it would be suicidal to accept some job that you really feel you couldn't do good work on. This town is unforgiving that way.

JB: I've heard you have a particular loathing for food photography.

PT: I've tried it a few times, but it's not for me. God help you if you ate that junk! You'd die instantly. I'm more into high-tech stuff.

JB: Well, you've certainly got quite a setup here for that sort of work.

PT: When we came here in 1967, this place was a shell. There was no balcony here. We gutted it and built a nice little studio. We've hung out here ever since. I love this place. It's not really big. This isn't a factory. When we do a big shoot, we rent a film studio. You can mess it up and do whatever you want.

JB: *Your* studio looks very well organized.

PT: Looks are deceiving. We're in the process of spring-cleaning. You open something up, and it's a can of worms. Literally. You reach in, and it's squirming. Whoa! You say to yourself, "I've been looking for this! And doesn't that belong over there?"

JB: Do you have a typical routine for setting up a photo session here?

PT: We have a very definite routine for that. We're not a shine 'em up and grind 'em out type studio. We try to service the client in a special way. We test prior to the shoot, so if I were shooting tomorrow, we'd test the lights tonight. We try to minimize all risks. Not only that, but it means we can give the art director something to look at when he comes by. We can project it onto the screen, and he can say, "Gee, I like this," and, "Can you change this a little bit?"

JB: What cameras and lenses do you use?

PT: Nikons exclusively.

JB: Why not a larger format?

PT: Well, I have to take that back. I do on occasion use a larger format when I'm working with multiple elements or special effects, mainly because we send it out to a lab for assembly, and it makes it a little easier for them. But that's rather rare. I find the combination of Nikon lenses and Kodachrome 25 to be excellent. One other thing, in New York, we have the wonderful advantage of New York Colorworks—and this is an undisguised plug. They offer push- or pull-processing, and even change color for you. About a year ago, we were shooting in a big studio on the West Side. It was a very expensive shoot—about $100,000. We set up and discovered we needed more light, but didn't have the time to double up on the lights, so I said, "Let's just push that film." We did tests, figured out what we wanted, and the lab took care of the problem. It saved us a lot of money because we would have been hanging lights until midnight, dealing with double shadows and all sorts of things.

JB: You're often quoted as saying that, for you, taking the photograph is only the very first step. What typically happens next?

PT: In the old days, the late fifties and early sixties, I used to filter things on the spot. But let's say I used a red filter, then came back and said, "Gee, I don't think that red works." I'm in a lot of trouble. So I started shooting everything normally. I might do a few frames with a filter to remind myself that this should have a heavy blue or a heavy whatever. But if you start in neutral and then go into the optical printer, to the second generation, which is our finish, then you have the option of using any filter. You're never stuck.

JB: You often do much more than add a color filter to an image though. Many of your futuristic images, like *Earthrise* and *Twin Planets,* are montages.

PT: That's right. I often shoot things with a black background, so I can use them in an assembled photograph later on. [He points down the length of the balcony, to where a double-tiered slide projector system has been set up.] We use that for overlays, to position and size

149

the various elements and to give us a rough idea of the final image. We project a very complicated grid with latitude, longitude—the whole works—onto the screen and take a Polaroid of the screen for a record. When we're ready to assemble, we use the same grid on the optical printer so everything will be positioned perfectly.

JB: I understand you're a science fiction fan. Do you have a favorite author?

PT: I love Arthur Clark.

JB: Have any particular writers or works inspired your photography?

PT: Not really. Science fiction has been an inspiration in general. It gave me a lot of ideas for montages. When we worked on Spielberg's *Close Encounters* poster, they came to us because we were doing this sort of thing.

JB: You're probably best known for your futuristic imagery. Pete Turner and high-tech are virtually synonymous in art directors' minds. Is it ever frustrating to be so typecast?

PT: No, I like that best. It's fun to travel in your imagination.

JB: At one time, you were part of a cooperative venture to promote color photography as an art—when you opened the Space Gallery with Jay Maisel and Ernst Haas. Since then, you haven't done much exhibiting yourself.

PT: No, none whatsoever. If I'm asked to be part of an exhibit, I'll say yes, but I don't actively seek out exhibitions. I *am* printing though—making units of fifty dye transfers. They're not on the market. I consider them sort of a legacy for my family. It's not a cheap venture, to say the least. We're in the process of making gifts to a very few museums. For instance, the Metropolitan accepted a selection of what I consider to be my best work for their permanent collection. That was one of Weston Naef's last gestures.

JB: Do you find that many museums and galleries still have a prejudice against color work?

PT: Yes, it's unfortunate. Admittedly, there are problems with color. If you print on inferior material, it's going to fade. But dye transfers, and apparently Cibachromes, are fairly archival in dark storage, with good humidity controls. All color under light will fade eventually. Paintings fade, and they get dirty and the varnish cracks. I'm more worried about the paper and emulsions holding up than the dyes fading, and for exhibitions, if you don't use ultraviolet light, no problem.

JB: You've been a professional photographer for close to thirty years. How have you managed to maintain your energy and enthusiasm, not to mention imagination, for so long?

PT: I don't have to get up at 4:00 a.m. and work until 2:00 a.m. because I surround myself with a really good management team. My studio manager, unfortunately for him, takes the brunt of that kind of thing. I see myself as more of an advisor or director. We operate more like a film studio here than like a still photography studio. I feel you can waste yourself if you stick your nose into everything. John has complete freedom to make his own decisions. I've done that with all my people. If you don't give a person responsibility, you take away his soul. You ask why most of them got to be successful? The trick is to say, "Here you go, buddy. It's all yours."

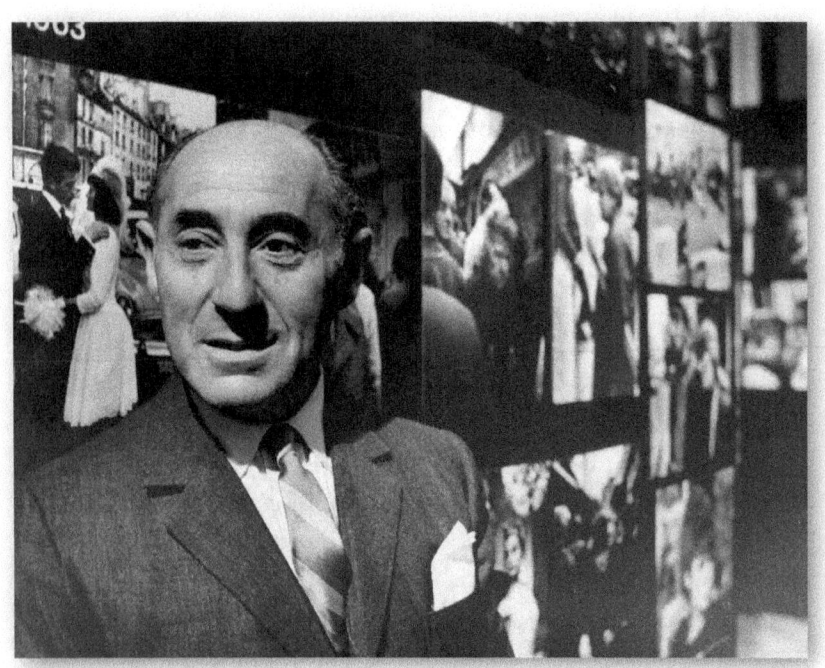

Photo by Tony Spina

ALFRED EISENSTAEDT (1898–1995)

The Affable Observer

Published March/April 1986

Nice and easy has always been photojournalist Alfred Eisenstaedt's style. For almost forty years, he traveled the world for *Life* magazine, collecting photographs (and autographs) of the famous and powerful. This made *him* famous, too. However, there's much more to his life than *Life*.

Alfred Eisenstaedt gets up at five o'clock every morning. He eats breakfast, and then walks to the corner newsstand, where he buys a copy of the *New York Times*. Even before it became his business, Eisenstaedt was drawn to current events, be they political, cultural, or scientific. "I am interested in everything—even whether or not a cockroach has hair on its head," he laughs.

By nine thirty, Eisenstaedt is in his office, a windowless warren just a stone's throw from the *Life* photo lab on the twenty-eighth floor of Manhattan's Time & Life Building. His office walls and a good portion of the floor are taken up by industrial shelving crammed with yellow Kodak boxes full of his prints.

Wherever there's space, Eisenstaedt has hung some of the photographs he likes best. Among them are several large prints of Marlene Dietrich, Sophia Loren—one of his favorite subjects—and his late wife Kathy, a woman Eisenstaedt says kept their marriage happy by her adherence to the simple motto, "First *Life,* then wife." High above a tiny bulletin board layered with scraps of paper hangs the American Society of Magazine Photographers' Lifetime Achievement Award, given to him in 1978 when he was seventy-nine.

Now eighty-seven, Eisenstaedt says his long, happy career and a lifetime of good habits are responsible for his durability and productivity. He doesn't drink or smoke. Until sciatica made it painful, he exercised regularly, carrying a pedometer with him on his frequent travels.

But he has one regret: "It's only too bad that I wasn't born fifty years later. Today, everything is done with so much technique. In my time, technique didn't matter. If I was younger, then I would have different cameras, different outfits—strobes, cables, assistants. I never worked with an assistant. I had a very good time, looking back, but today's photographers are terrific—don't you think so?"

If Eisenstaedt envies the careers of modern photographers, many are just as envious of his. He worked for years as an Associated Press photographer in pre-World War II Europe, but the cynosure of his career was his decades at *Life*. Along with Margaret Bourke-White, Peter Stackpole, and Tom McAvoy, Eisenstaedt was one of *Life*'s original staff of photographers, and he stayed with *Life* from the magazine's first issue in 1936 until the influential weekly ceased publication in 1972. Even after that, he kept his office at Time Incorporated, and his name went back on *Life*'s masthead when it started up again as a monthly in 1978.

Life's influence was tremendous. When it began publication on the tail end of the Depression, radio, newspapers, and newsreels had piqued people's curiosity about the world at a time when travel was prohibitive for all but the very rich and very adventurous. As would television decades later, *Life* allowed its readers to become armchair voyeurs and adventurers. Millions of Americans and Europeans fanned copies of the big picture weekly across their coffee tables and picked it up again and again to look at its photographs of the mighty and meek, the fortunate and the unfortunate, politicians, soldiers, movie stars, scientists, socialites, and shack dwellers. It shaped its readers' opinions on a score of topics, and it took this responsibility very seriously. "We thought we ran the world," remembers one editor. When Ed Sullivan invited *Life*'s publisher, Henry Luce, onto his show and asked him to explain *Life*'s philosophy, Luce's answer sounded like a pledge: "We believe that human life has a purpose, and our job is to show individual people and nations working out that purpose in freedom and justice for all."

The operative word was *show*; it was photographs more than words that gave *Life* its power. Among working photographers, a *Life* assignment, or better yet, a slot on staff, was highly coveted. Those who made it knew they'd arrived at the inner sanctum of the only club worth joining. There were photojournalists and there were *Life Photographers*. "We were an elite corps," says Eisenstaedt.

Life's photographers went everywhere and saw everything. "I was traveling all the time," remembers Eisenstaedt. "From one assignment to another. I came home sometimes at 1:00 a.m., but I didn't stay at home. I went to *Life,* always something else coming up—all the time. I did more than 2,500 assignments and ninety-two covers. Once, I had three covers in a month."

Henry Luce, a man given to definitive pronouncements, often called Eisenstaedt the father of photojournalism. Eisenstaedt more accurately calls himself the son. However much Luce would have liked to believe that *Life* was the first picture magazine worth counting, photojournalism was in fact born in Europe, long before *Life,* and enjoyed a period of exceptional prosperity in Germany as Eisenstaedt was growing up.

Alfred Eisenstaedt was born in Dirschau, West Prussia (now part of Poland), on December 6, 1898. When he was seven, his father sold the department store he owned there, and moved his family to Berlin.

On Eisenstaedt's fourteenth birthday, his uncle gave him his first camera, an Eastman Kodak Folding Camera No. 3, loaded with roll film. He immediately took to his new hobby: "I took lots of pictures of unimportant things."

In 1916, when Eisenstaedt was seventeen, he set aside his camera and his formal education when he was drafted into the German army. One of the *Kindersoldaten* who were recruited as Germany's reserves were depleted, Eisenstaedt served on the Western Front. His tour ended when on April 12, 1918, during a bombardment 125 miles from Verdun, he was hit in both knees with shrapnel from a British artillery shell. He remembers the moment to the minute: 4:10 p.m. He was the only survivor in his battery.

Eisenstaedt had seen all he wanted of war. Later, many of his colleagues at *Life,* notably Carl Mydans and W. Eugene Smith, built their reputations in part on their war reportage. For a time, *Life* ran a school for combat photographers. But, while Eisenstaedt has gone to unusual, even dangerous lengths to obtain some of his photographs—once lashing himself to the flying bridge of a ship during a hurricane to record the storm's fury—for the most part he steered clear of manmade danger and never again ventured onto a battlefield.

Back in Berlin, his knees on the mend, Eisenstaedt took a job as a salesman of belts and buttons. "A very bad one," he says. For the next eight years, this was his primary occupation, but photography filled his leisure time.

One of the pictures that hang in Eisenstaedt's office is of a lone tennis player, her racket drawn back preparatory to serving. Except for the vague gray folds of her tunic, she's a softly defined silhouette in the photo's upper right hand quadrant. Her shadow stretches long to the lower left corner. The salt and pepper textures of the tennis court fill the rest of the print.

Eisenstaedt took this photograph in 1926. He made a contact print and showed it to a friend "who also dabbled in photography a little bit." His friend suggested he enlarge it. "I said, 'What's enlarging? I've never heard of enlarging.' I went to his home and he showed me a contraption mounted on a wall—a wooden box with a frosted bulb inside. This opened my eyes to the possibilities of photography."

The technology for commercially printing large quantities of photographs was available as early as the 1850s, but it wasn't until the halftone process was perfected in 1880 that photographs and type could be printed together economically. At the same time, the invention of small handheld cameras made photography an efficient and effective newsgathering tool. Photographs began to appear with increasing regularity in newspapers, especially in Sunday supplements. Germany was the leader in the new form of communication that became known as photojournalism. In his *History of Photography*, Beaumont Newhall reports that by 1930, there were more illustrated magazines in Germany than anywhere else in the world, with combined circulations of five million per week and twenty million readers.

Eisenstaedt enlarged the photograph of the tennis player and sold it to the weekly magazine *Der Welt Spiegel* for three marks, or about twelve dollars. A few weeks later, he sold a second photograph to the same magazine. Its editor suggested that he study the work of Erich Salomon, one of the period's most famous photojournalists. Eisenstaedt already knew Salomon's photography. "I admired him tremendously," he writes in *Eisenstaedt on Eisenstaedt*. "He was like a god to me. I knew that Salomon used an Ermanox camera, and I bought one too. After that, I was not interested in anything else. I was a fanatic about photography. I still am."

On December 3, 1929, at the age of thirty, Eisenstaedt said good-bye to the belt and button business and became a full-time photographer for Pacific and Atlantic Photos (which became the Associated Press in 1931), for whom he'd already been freelancing. He had the ambivalent blessings of his boss, who knew Eisenstaedt's talents did not lie in sales, but doubted that a decent living could be made with a camera. "The idea of photography for a living was as new as flying," Eisenstaedt remembers.

Less than a week later, he was on his way to Stockholm to photograph Thomas Mann accepting the Nobel Prize for literature. After that, he traveled throughout England and Europe, dragging hundreds of pounds of heavy glass plates for the big cameras favored by his new employers and wearing suits and formal clothing specially reinforced to accommodate the plates and their steel holders. Photojournalism was not yet a truly portable profession, nor could photojournalists get away with the casual attire of today.

The smaller Ermanox eventually changed Eisenstaedt's style, and he said, "It started me on a more candid kind of photography." He photographed movie stars, musicians, statesmen, and ordinary people at work and at play. "I was elated because I was with so many people who were famous in the world's eyes. Very few people did what I did at the time. My photographs appeared everywhere because I was with the Associated Press, and they sold to every magazine."

In 1932, Eisenstaedt began traveling with a 6 x 9 cm Miroflex and the 35mm Leica he would favor for the rest of his career. He went to St. Moritz to photograph high society and was a presence at the many political conferences held during the post war years as politicians met to repair the damage of World War I. At Geneva in 1933, Eisenstaedt caught Hitler's minister of propaganda, Joseph Goebbels, as he glared suspiciously at the camera. Later, Goebbels signed Eisenstaedt's autograph book. In 1934, after being arrested and held for several hours until his AP credentials were verified, he photographed Hitler's first meeting with Mussolini. At President von Hindenberg's funeral, he photographed Hitler wearing the uniform of the Fuhrer for the first time.

With Hitler's supremacy came the demise of German photojournalism. One by one the German picture presses closed down. Then, as now, Eisenstaedt says he was apolitical, and if he objected to anything about a subject, he ignored it in favor of objectivity. This is probably why by 1935 he was one of two photographers with official permission to photograph in Germany. But when the Berlin Bureau of the Associated Press disbanded, Eisenstaedt, like many of his compatriots, immigrated to the United States.

Still employed by the Associated Press, Eisenstaedt did not want for work. He photographed for *Town & Country*, tried his hand at a few fashion assignments, and contributed to the dummies of an experimental Time publication called "Project X." "They saw my pictures and said, 'This is the kind of photography we want.'" On November 23, 1936, the mysterious Project X was revealed to the public as *Life* magazine, and Eisenstaedt began his extended tenure there.

"At *Life*, everybody was an individualist. You could do anything you wanted to do. You had no timetable. You could stay out as long as you needed, but I always tried to do it as fast as possible because I wanted to do another assignment. I was a fanatic. I was always jumping from one assignment to another. The more I worked, the happier I felt."

Eisenstaedt claimed the cover of the second issue of *Life* with a story about West Point. By now, he was using the Leica almost exclusively and a Rolleiflex intermittently. He did photo essays on universities and hospitals and covered the home front during World War II, beginning with a series of heart-wrenching pictures of women taking leave of their men at New York City's Pennsylvania Station and culminating with the famous VJ-Day shot of a jubilant sailor smooching a passing nurse in Times Square.

But as time passed, Eisenstaedt eased away from photographing places and events. The photography of the famous became his specialty. In this role, Eisenstaedt adhered to the Golden Rule. A congenial man who always asks for an autograph at the end of a session, Eisenstaedt has never seen any point in exploiting his subjects' human frailties. The pleasant countenances he submitted to *Life* are proof of his belief that you don't repay with unkindness the kindness of a celebrity who finds time for a photographer in a busy schedule.

Everyone asks Eisenstaedt if he was ever intimidated by the fame of his subjects. He likes to answer with advice given to him by *Life* photo editor Wilson Hicks when he assigned him to Hollywood—even though this took place well into his career. "He said, 'Alfred, don't be intimidated by all these beauty queens. You are a king in your profession. You're very good.' And this has stuck with me."

"I treat everybody normally," he says. "When you meet famous and important people they don't *like* to be treated like you look in awe of them." Eisenstaedt knows this firsthand, because there came a time when he was a celebrity in his own right and he experienced adulation. "I hate it," he says. "What does a photographer compare to a composer, a painter, a surgeon? Nothing. People think I conquered the world. No. I'm just a photographer, pure and simple. I admire all the greats who have done so much for the world. But a photographer? What does he do?"

Eisenstaedt keeps up an easy banter throughout photo sessions to set his subjects at ease and being widely read he can find common ground for a conversation with anyone from movie stars to scientists to statespersons. He steers clear of the controversial, however. "To photograph all these famous people, I have to be more diplomat than photographer. And then it helps that I have very little equipment. I have sometimes one or two lamps along and work alone. Very often people say, 'Are you finished already?' I was always known as an under shooter."

Eisenstaedt's powers of diplomacy were stretched to the limit when he met Ernest Hemingway in 1952, an assignment he names unfailingly as his most difficult. "Papa" Hemingway was living in Havana. He greeted Eisenstaedt with a gin and tonic in hand, wearing only a pair of frayed and faded shorts. From the start, Hemingway was irascible. He complained about *Life*'s fee of $40,000, saying it was too low. He became enraged when Eisenstaedt asked him to put on a shirt, demanding to know why he should cover himself when so many famous actresses had loved his body just the way it was. Eisenstaedt says he responded by matching machismo with machismo. He pulled up his sleeve and asked Hemingway for a very sharp pocketknife, boasting that he would bounce it off his biceps. "Look, Mary, he's a little Papa," Hemingway said to his wife. Eventually, he put on his shirt.

For all his difficulties with Hemingway—and there were more in ensuing days—Eisenstaedt returned to photograph him again the following year. "I have no trouble going back to people I have photographed because I am never obnoxious," he says.

One favorite subject he photographed many times over the years was Sophia Loren, of whom he did five of his ninety-two *Life* covers. She always asked for approval and never rejected a shot. He remembers the first time he photographed her: "My editor called me and said, 'Eisie, we have a very good assignment for you, a very interesting assignment.' When he told me what it was, I said, 'I'll be ready in fifteen minutes.' The next day I left for Rome. We clicked right away. That's most important. I was for years a part of the family."

Eisenstaedt was an unabashed fan. Early in his career, an AP writer with whom he was working suggested that he collect the signatures of his famous subjects, and since then, he has filled a score of autograph books with their scribbles. He locates one of the more recent books among his piles of papers. There are the marks of Norman Rockwell, Pierre Trudeau, Saul Bellow, Jacques Henri-Lartigue, Anna Freud, Mikhail Baryshnikov, Leni Riefenstahl, Glenn Gould, and Yousuf Karsh. Most also have scrawled their thanks for a pleasant photo session.

As much as he enjoyed photographing celebrities, Eisenstaedt's favorite assignments were few and far between: "Portraiture and news photography are fine, but I always liked nature assignments best. But the editors told me, 'There are many people who can do nature, but there are very few who can do what you do.' And so I was stuck with people."

Eisenstaedt's constant travels and his workaholism precluded serious romantic attachments until he met Alma Kathy Kaye in 1947. Kathy, a product of a traditional English upbringing in colonial Capetown, South Africa, worked for her sister, who owned a candy store on Fifth Avenue. They courted for a year and nine months and were married in 1949 when Eisenstaedt was fifty.

Eisenstaedt and his bride spent their wedding night riding the rails on the Twentieth Century Limited, en route to Hollywood. When they arrived, they went from the train directly to the set of Gene Kelly's *On the Town*. "It was fantastic for my wife," says Eisenstaedt. "Can you imagine? She met Gregory Peck, Robert Taylor—everybody!" The Eisenstaedts were in Hollywood for seven weeks while he photographed movie stars for *Life*. "That was our honeymoon," he says, adding without regret, "They never published one picture."

Eisenstaedt continued to travel and work, with his wife's understanding and encouragement. "She was a great help to me spiritually. She gave me peace of mind," he says. And so 1972 was doubly tragic for Eisenstaedt. On December 8, two days after his seventy-third birthday, *Life* discontinued publication. "We thought the end of the world had come. It was very bad." That year too, after twenty-two years of marriage, Kathy died.

Eisenstaedt kept busy. He worked for other Time publications and obtained an agent. He headed a photo expedition to Brazil—"a horrible experience"—and worked for the British Tourist Authority. From 1969 to 1976, he published a book a year, and every other year thereafter. In 1979, he returned to Germany to take a second look at some of the sites he'd photographed in the thirties.

In 1978, *Life* was revitalized, but Eisenstaedt says, "I don't work so much for the new *Life*. I don't work so much anymore lately. Travel is a little difficult for me."

Nonetheless, in 1985, the latest of his eleven books of photography, *Eisenstaedt on Eisenstaedt*, was published, and in 1986, "Eisenstaedt and company," a major exhibition with over ninety photographs—many of them recent—opened in London. Clearly, for Eisenstaedt, working a little and working a lot are relative.

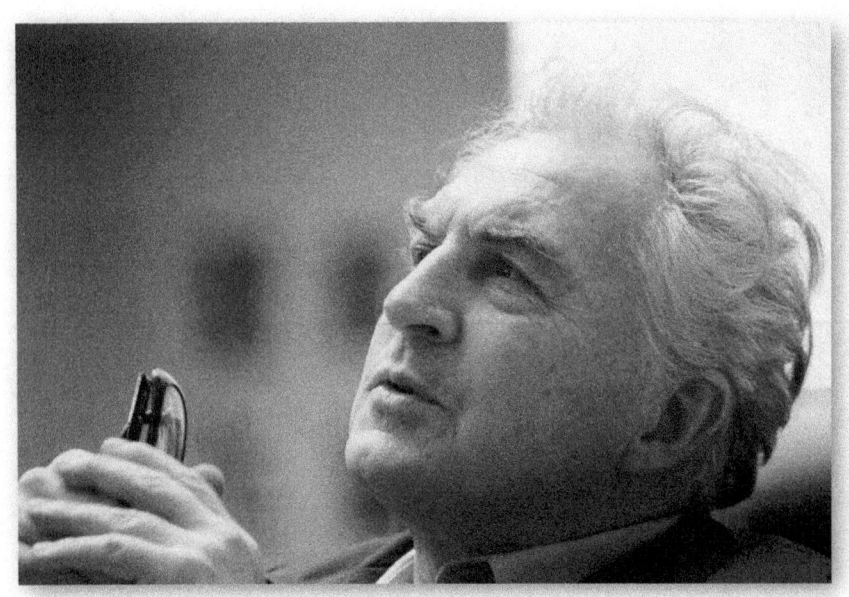

Photo by Mark Harmel

ERNST HAAS (1921–1986)

A Conversation

Published May/June 1986

E rnst Haas, honored by *Popular Photography* in 1958 as one of the world's ten greatest photographers, is often described as a free spirit. A native of Vienna, Haas has lived in New York City since 1950, but you're as likely to find him in Europe, the Orient, or even Marlboro Country as in his midtown apartment just down the street from Carnegie Hall. At sixty-four, he's a successful commercial photographer, one of the three to photograph the iconic Marlboro man, but his Leicaflex certainly isn't always trained on client-mandated subjects. His book *The Creation,* a collection of photographs that demand an almost visceral response, is one of the most popular books of photography ever published. He's also the author of *In America, In Germany,* and *Himalayan Pilgrimage,* and the creator of a series of lush, thought-provoking audiovisual presentations.

JB: You've had exhibits at a number of prestigious venues, including New York City's Museum of Modern Art and Cologne's Photokina. But now you rarely exhibit your photographs in the traditional manner—by hanging them on the wall. You put them in books, or show them in your audiovisual presentations. Why is that?

EH: I was never really happy with the end result of hanging a photograph on the wall. This form of exhibition is an old hang-up from painting. We're conditioned to think that if something is extraordinary, then it should be hung on the wall. Photography comes from seeing. It's a living experience. It's a process. I like to present it that way.

JB: What do you mean by process?

EH: Picasso's work is a good example of process. He attains a metamorphosis of a theme by exploring it in, say, two hundred pictures. What I do with photography is similar except that I like to show the process. The audiovisual presentation is a way to express motion in time. I love that it is not one picture after another, as it is in a gallery, but the melding of two images to create a third image. You can really juxtapose anything with anything and leave it to the audience to interpret it. And they have to participate in an audiovisual. I always notice that at my audiovisual presentation more people sit like this [Haas sits forward, peering intently at an invisible screen], than this, like they do at a movie [he sits back in his seat, assuming a mildly interested expression].

JB: How long have you been making audiovisual presentations?

EH: About ten years. It began when I visited the island of San Michele, in Venice, where the dead are buried. Each grave has a little photograph. Some go back to 1850. But the sun is so strong that it starts to influence the photograph, and because the chemicals were not so pure as they are now, very often the images start to solarize and eventually disappear. In a way, it's a second death. Suddenly, a nose is missing and an eye and a mouth. Then there's just the outline of a head. I loved it. But how do you show this? Then I learned there was a technique where you could blend one image against another *and* set it all to music. This I liked because I've always been fascinated with music, and I always wanted to combine the two mediums, which don't need translation and are international.

After that, I discovered I had begun to photograph for my audiovisuals. It became a completely different way of seeing. You begin to think in terms of sequences. But when you stop and think about it, even with a book or a portfolio, you still often work toward a theme, and you show variations of it. I work in a fluid process. That's why an 8 x 10 camera is not for me. I work unconsciously. I love to be surprised by myself. The more you work with a bigger camera, the more you become static. You are no longer within flux, and I love this flux—the fluidity of the process.

JB: Have you tried anything similar with video?

EH: It's too small, and the image isn't as good. It doesn't have the volume. When you blow up a good 35mm—that's when you really start to feel something. You see so many different nuances. Also, I notice with audiovisuals that people never see one totally. You show it to them a second time, and they say, "You changed a lot!" But I haven't changed *anything*.

JB: I've been struck by the advantage audiovisuals give the photographer in choosing how long viewers will look at each image. This is something the photographer has no control over with a book or gallery show.

EH: I wouldn't hold one against the other. Both are totally different experiences. The audiovisual is in itself a very beautiful new art form.

JB: In addition to creating audiovisuals, you've published a number of books, including *The Creation*. It was first published in 1971, and a second edition was published in 1983. How do you account for its phenomenal success?

EH: It was a surprise for me. I didn't expect it. I thought I'd sell maybe twenty thousand, but never a quarter of a million and more. But I was always interested in different creation myths, going back to my earliest childhood. I think that where we come from and where we go and the meaning of it all are elemental dilemmas for all of us. We're instinctively fascinated with these myths and drawn to them. In *The Creation*, I tried to illustrate this through photographs of the seasons or the elements or of wildlife. And whenever I give a seminar, I always advise my students to try to photograph these myths, because we all have our own ideas about the creation.

JB: You've changed some of the images for the second edition.

EH: I changed them because some of the original images were damaged and because I had some images that I thought were better than the originals. You know, it isn't finished when the book is published. You keep on photographing it. When the publishers came and asked me if I wanted to do a second edition, I was very happy. It meant I could redo some text and pictures. I am only unhappy the second edition is not printed as well as the first. The first one was printed with the gravure process. The second is offset. In gravure, you can get a velvet color, which I need. I don't like a glossy color very much. A book is always a compromise. You can get *this* color, but then you lose some of *that* color, you know? This is why I always go to be there when they start printing, to decide where to make the compromises.

JB: The notes about the photographs in *The Creation* are a testament to the amount of traveling you've done. There are photos taken in the Amazon, India, Iceland, the Galapagos, Uganda…

EH: Last year was the worst. I was away almost eight and a half months. That includes four months in Japan. These last two months, I was in seven countries. It becomes insane.

JB: Were you traveling on assignment?

EH: Yes, I took on quite a few commercial assignments last year, so I can do my own work this year and can leave New York knowing my children will be taken care of. I can always live on very little.

JB: Do you pick and choose your assignments these days?

EH: Well, I have assignments that I like, but there's an interesting thing that happens that I've often talked to other well-known photographers about. You can get such a good reputation that almost nobody calls you. They assume you would never agree to work for them, or they think you'll be too expensive. So they hire someone less well known and ask *him* to do the photography à la so and so. That means it's not always an advantage to have a good reputation. For me, they probably think I'm too old, since I've been in the business so long. "He must be at least eighty!"

JB: If you didn't travel so much on assignment, would you travel anyway?

EH: Maybe it sounds snobbish, but I don't really travel. I feel this is all one territory, one world. I have friends in India, and I go there, and it's like home. I go to Japan, and it's like home.

When I first started traveling, it took seven hours to get from Vienna to Innsbruck. Today, I can go from New York to Europe in less than seven hours. So I don't feel that I'm transporting myself in any extraordinary way by going to Japan or India, and I don't feel that I'm seeing anything extraordinarily new. At my age, I like to go places where I've been and dig deeper. It's too late to be surprised by a new place.

And I like places that are small. People say I should go to see China, but it's too big. I'd rather delve into the small and make something big—something magnificent and deep and profound—than delve into something I can only lick and tickle a little bit. That's why I like Japan so much. I'm working on a book about it.

JB: You've written that you believe a photographer's normal development should go from black-and-white to color as a kind of natural progression.

EH: Yes. It's like when you learn to paint, you should be able to draw, and if you compose music, you should know the notes, so you can make a sketch of your music. I have a great love for black-and-white photography. I spent almost fifteen years working with it. But good color is much more particular. I don't think it's black-and-white versus color, good versus bad. There is mediocre versus masterful in both mediums. I have great admiration for photographers like Cartier-Bresson and Edward Weston who worked only in black-and-white.

JB: And it was Cartier-Bresson who taught you about the decisive moment, which is so important in your own work.

EH: Yes, I would never have known about the decisive moment in color if Henri hadn't defined it in black-and-white. What is most remarkable about photography is not the miracle of reproduction, but that you can hold a moment. This had never before happened in the history of art. Before, all our moments were idealized moments, all beautifully composed. The psychological structure of the decisive moment in color is similar to black-and-white. You see a moment of depth and react with a certain *pah!* that comes from the stomach. It doesn't come from thought but from feeling. But it's not the same as in black-and-white. Each requires a different way of seeing. In color, there is more happening, more to balance and juggle and more that can go wrong.

JB: Was your early black-and-white work documentary in nature?

EH: When I started photographing right after the war, my work was very abstract. I took some of this work to Switzerland to show the editor of the magazine *Du*. He said, "How strange. Here's a young man from a war-torn city like Vienna, and he photographs in the abstract, instead of documenting the ruins." But, you see, I grew up in the ruins. For me, they were nothing extraordinary. Then he showed me the work of a photographer named Werner Bischof. I was so impressed! The editor said, "Do you want to meet him?" I said, "No, I want to go back to Vienna and photograph!" Almost two years later, Robert Capa invited me to Paris to join Magnum along with Bischof. That's when I met him.

JB: That's about the same time you declined an offer to join *Life*'s staff.

EH: Yes. At the time, it was considered like a fantastic part in a Hollywood movie, but I'm not made for staff. I had been with *Life* photographers, and I never envied them. They were a pampered lot, and spoiled, although they worked very hard. I eventually left Magnum too. I love them all. They're very nice. But I wanted to be by myself.

JB: You've often said that when you were working in black-and-white you reached a point when you were longing for color. What was the turning point?

EH: It was about 1949. You see, the war was a gray time. There was no *courage* for color. The houses were gray, the clothes were gray, the food was gray, the mentality was gray—everything was gray. When peace broke out, color broke out too. People stared to paint everything.

I remember working for some Americans with teenagers who had socks ringed with many different colors. I thought they were the most beautiful things I'd ever seen, so I traded for a pair. The color fascinated me. Our society was so colorless. We didn't want to stand out, so we became gray to blend into the masses. Color to me meant, "Here I am! Look at me!" I come from a culture where the older you get, the grayer you get. A woman who is sixty should wear black. A man who is sixty wears dark gray or brown. Color is only for the children. It's not like that in this country.

JB: Did you start photographing in color before or after you came to New York?

EH: My first color story was a two-part series on New York City that was published in *Life*. It was a big event for color photography because *Life* was only using 4 x 5 color at that time. So 35mm was new to them. *National Geographic* had done it before—they always worked in 35mm. It was during this time when *Life* would send you out to shoot black-and-white *and* color at the same time. That became very difficult, and I tried to avoid it, because if you really see color, it's difficult to translate that into black-and-white.

JB: Jumping ahead a few years, you once opened a photo gallery with Jay Maisel and Pete Turner devoted exclusively to color photography. Why did it close?

EH: The Space Gallery. Yes. But color was very expensive, and it didn't succeed. It's such a pity, because now I think it might. The gap between color and black-and-white photography would be much smaller if we could make prints in color as well as we can in black-and-white. But we still can't. Type C is not really good color and Cibachrome is so-so. Dye transfer is really good color, but is so disproportionately expensive. With what I spend to make one dye transfer, I could make one hundred black-and-white prints. We have the best lenses and fantastic films right now, but we can't translate it, unless we project it.

JB: You mentioned earlier that it's too late to be surprised by new places. Do you think you've reached a point in your career where you're thinking in terms of summing up?

EH: Yes. At sixty-four, you have to begin thinking about how you want to conclude the cycle.

JB: In looking back over your work, is there anything that stands out as especially successful?

EH: Successful? I really don't know quite what that means. It's not that I want to be a snob, but my conclusion is not only concerned with photography. It goes beyond photography. This is what I teach in my seminars. Photography is a springboard. To see and to feel and to think and bring it together as a total experience—that, I think, is a conclusion.

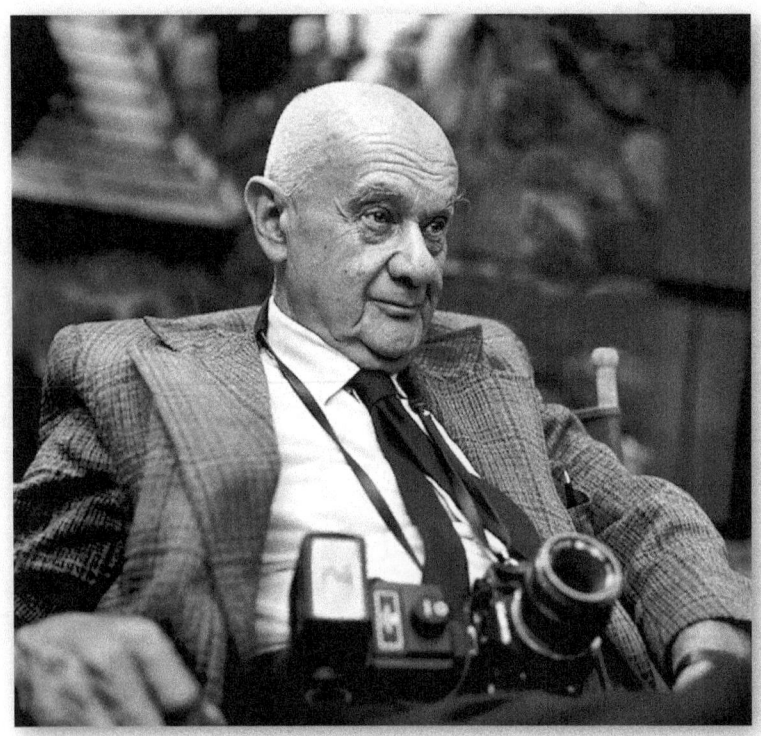

Photo by Andrew A. Skolnick

ROMAN VISHNIAC (1897–1990)

A People Remembered

Published July/August 1986

Warsaw, 1938. A young Jewish girl, dressed in an overlarge, too-thin coat, stands talking to an old man. Her right hand clutches her left. She cannot get work. Her parents are ill. The old man, her grandfather, whose own coat is worn but bulky, listens in mute sympathy. Nearby, unnoticed, Roman Vishniac presses the cable release that opens the shutter on his hidden camera. Over thirty-five years later, he remembers their conversation in the caption accompanying this image in his book, *A Vanished World,* and recounts what he learned about them after the war: "The grandfather died when he was seized by the Nazis, the granddaughter was shipped to a camp where she was raped and later gassed. An ordinary story."

Vishniac took this picture near the end of a six-year, five thousand-mile odyssey through Eastern Europe. Posing as a traveling salesman, he photographed the Jews who'd banded together in city ghettos and isolated mountain villages during centuries of persecution. He was convinced they would soon be exterminated. It was a courageous, and surely haunting, self-assignment. The disguise was necessary to escape the notice of the authorities, as well as his subjects, who believed photographs were graven images forbidden by God. It fooled the trustful, but not the suspicious. Vishniac was arrested countless times. Only two thousand of the sixteen thousand photographs he took between 1934 and 1939 were saved.

"It is a miracle that I am a survivor," says Vishniac, now eighty-eight. We're seated among teetering piles of books and boxes of prints in the dim study of his New York City apartment.

Vishniac's English, one of his nine languages, is still accented, although he's lived on New York's Upper West Side since 1940. He came by way of Berlin and before that Russia, where in 1897, he was born into a middle-class Russian/Jewish family. At seven, he took his first photographs through a microscope, the start of a lifelong fascination with photography and science that decades later would make him the world's foremost photomicrographer. At twenty-three, he earned an MD and a PhD in zoology at Moscow's Shanyavsky University—the first of twenty-two advanced degrees.

As we speak, Vishniac uses the word "miracle" often. He has been the recipient of quite a few. In his rebellious twenties, he demonstrated against the Kerensky government in Moscow. At one protest, the demonstrators were fired upon and nearly all killed. When it was quiet, Vishniac, shaken but spared, crawled out from under the bodies of his friends. Not long after, he was arrested and sentenced to death for treason. He was again miraculously reprieved, this time by the Russian Revolution, which began one half hour before his scheduled execution. Vishniac left Moscow for Berlin in 1920. He obtained exit visas for his family, but could not get one for himself, so he crossed the border in the dark hours of early morning, ducking gunfire and searchlights.

Many stories circulate about Vishniac's narrow escapes and self-described "iron nerves," but today he is sparing with his anecdotes, presumably saving them for an autobiography that's in progress. He's working simultaneously on a second book about Europe's prewar shtetl, tentatively titled *Life Before Death*. He also travels frequently at the invitation of organizations around the world. Since last year, the fortieth anniversary of the end of World War II, he's been especially popular.

Midway through our talk, he excuses himself to speak with a Swedish interviewer who is on a tighter schedule than mine. His second wife Edith, whom he married in 1947, comes in to keep me company. When Vishniac was awarded the George Eastman medal, he had it inscribed "Roman E. Vishniac." The "E" stands for Edith, out of gratitude for her enduring love and support, through good times and bad. "Every year it is like this," she says. "It is not easy for him. He has trouble sleeping. But he feels it is important."

Vishniac is now acclaimed for his photographs of Europe's martyred Jews, but it wasn't always so. Although a slim volume was published in 1947, his attempts to publish the photos elsewhere were not well received, and he says Jewish organizations tried to suppress them. Not until the eighties, with the publication of *A Vanished World,* was the world really ready to view such graphic evidence of what Hitler and his Nazis had destroyed.

During the intervening years, Vishniac worked as a portrait photographer and, after 1950, as a freelance photomicrographer. Now, in addition to various other pursuits, he lectures on "The Sources of Creativity" at New York's Pratt Institute. "I teach my students wisdom," he says.

JB: You began photographing the Jewish communities of Eastern and Central Europe in 1934, right after Hitler came to power. What made you decide to take on what you knew would be a difficult and dangerous task?

RV: I was certain that Hitler would kill as many Jews as he could. I decided to make a kind of monument of how these people lived. This is *A Vanished World.* The only other monuments that exist are the ashes of the burned people. I took all the photographs before the war. They are not of atrocities, but of a very difficult way of life.

JB: That early on, few people were willing to believe that Hitler posed such a threat. Why were you so certain he did?

RV: I read *Mein Kampf.* Hitler wrote that the Jewish question must be solved. I considered these words even more dangerous than if he'd said that he wanted to kill the Jews, because then he might not have succeeded. He succeeded by not telling the complete truth. People were arrested and sent to concentration camps, but they did not know at first that they would be murdered. Later, they were told, or they understood.

I read *Mein Kampf,* and then I spoke to the Nazis, trying to understand their psychology. I rented a uniform and spoke to them as if I was one of them. I asked, "Why should we kill?" They said that when they got an order to murder, they'd murder.

JB: Did you set out to do all the photography alone, or did you look for a partner or assistant?

RV: At the time there was a special Jewish photo organization. It had been formed when Jews were thrown out of other established photo clubs because they weren't Aryans. We called it *Temunah*, Hebrew for "picture." The best photographer of the time, Mr. Fritz Eshen, was our president. When I spoke to them of the necessity of saving the memory of the Jews, everybody told me that it was insanity. It was too dangerous. I would be thrown in prison, or worse. Nobody wanted to help me. Instead, they warned me not to do it.

Then I spoke to the great Jewish historian Senen Dubnov. He wrote a many-volume history of the Jews. It's been translated into every language. When I brought him the pictures of my first trip to Poland, he cried out, "This is the greatest breakthrough!" He embraced me and kissed me, he was so excited.

The sad story is that he was murdered in the gas chamber in 1942. So were the people who warned me not to do dangerous things. They died in spite of being careful. So this is something that cannot be predicted. I always felt that I must do the best for the Jewish people, and God must take care of me.

JB: Did the people you photographed know their lives were in danger?

RV: They were afraid. But like most people, they were optimistic. They thought, because they were religious, that a miracle would happen—that Almighty God would not let them or their children die. It was very tragic for me to be with them and hear their questions. I didn't tell them that I was afraid for them, and that was why I was there. I told everyone I was a traveling salesman. I hid my photo equipment under my clothes. Nobody knew I took pictures.

JB: Where did you hide your camera?

RV: It was here [he points to his neck], covered with a scarf. The lens looked through a buttonhole. I never took two pictures, only one, because it was difficult to get film.

JB: What kind of camera did you use?

RV: I had the original Rolleiflex. It was primitive; it was marked three feet, seven feet, fifteen feet, and infinity. I never focused. I had a cable release in my right hand. My film was ASA 16. I did not breathe during the exposure, sometimes for five, six seconds.

JB: Did your subjects ever think it was odd that you stopped speaking or moving for prolonged periods of time?

RV: I don't think so. They had other problems. It was possible they thought I had some trouble breathing. They were not suspicious people. In this time, if I knocked on a door, nobody asked me, "What do you want?" Instead they asked, "Where are you coming from? What's new there?" They didn't close the door in my face. There was nothing to steal. They didn't have anything. This was a life of saints. I was very touched, being so close to them, seeing and experiencing their struggles—their efforts to get better education for their children and fighting poor health. It was very touching, very moving. I never heard of a divorce. They lived a really normal, good life. They didn't try to make money dishonestly. Everything was hard for them. The Poles didn't dare murder very many Jews, but they made life impossible economically and socially. The Jews defended themselves by working harder.

JB: Was the Rolleiflex the only camera you used?

RV: I also had the original Leica. And I often had a movie camera with me. But only the rejects remain. People look at these rejects with great excitement, because the people are living in movies.

JB: How did you get your photographic supplies?

RV: I had to return to Berlin. In one store, the clerk gave me the film if I paid two or three times the normal price. He was not certain that I was a Jew, but he certainly understood that there was a reason

I permitted him to overcharge me. That was normal, for me to pay more, because he took a risk. Later, he would have to prove that he sold only to Aryans.

JB: How did you develop your film?

RV: I carried the developing chemicals with me and would take a little chair down to the river on moonless nights. Moonlight spoils the film. But in good weather, you have all the stars, and they do not affect the images. To wash the negatives, I walked into the river, holding the film. And the times I was stopped by the police or in prison, my interrogators also developed much of my film, in order to find out if I was a spy.

JB: A spy?

RV: It was forbidden to take pictures of poverty and suffering, because it would make these places look unattractive to tourists and damage the economy. Those who took such pictures were thought to be spies and were imprisoned and put to death.

JB: How was it that prison guards knew how to develop film?

RV: They did not know how to do it, really. They used paper developer—what we call hydroquinone—because it is much quicker. But it is very harsh. It makes negatives that are difficult to print. I had to bleach them to redevelop them, and I had many problems because they didn't wash the negatives between developing and fixing. I got spotty results. I printed the negatives myself and worked three years on the prints for this book. Some of them took a week, because I had to use ferricyanide to get more details into the prints.

JB: How many times were you arrested?

RV: Many times. I was thrown in prison eleven times. Later, when I was miraculously released, I bribed them to get the film and equipment back.

In prison, they put me in complete darkness to break my resistance. I didn't know what time it was. I did not know if I would get another meal or if they would forget me for six months, then take out my remains and throw them to the dogs. In spite of this, when they released me, I began photographing the next day.

Even when I was sitting for a long time in the darkness, I was in a good mood. Melancholy is death, so you have to be in a good mood and expect a miracle to happen. It didn't always. We know that six and a half million were murdered in spite of their hopes. But we are trying now to keep alive the memory of the Holocaust. That's very important. It must never happen again.

JB: Your family was in Berlin during many of these years. Didn't your comings and goings attract the authorities' attention? Wasn't it dangerous to keep slipping in and out like that?

RV: It was very dangerous. For two hundred marks a month, I bought a friend in the police. When I left Berlin, I left my family enough money so they would get by until my return. But I did not give my wife [his first wife, Luta] any information. I did not write her letters. Everything was too risky. I was always alone. I had no assistance. This would be impossible. I never had powerful or rich friends. My own friends tried to prevent me from doing what I wanted to do. But you cannot predict what will happen. It is destiny.

JB: How were you supporting yourself and financing your photographic expeditions?

RV: I went by foot, or sometimes by railroad, which was not expensive. I was with people who were very poor. Money was not a question.

JB: But meanwhile, you had to take care of your family, pay bribes, and purchase materials.

RV: What is most important comes first. If you want it and have to have it, then you get it.

JB: When did you leave Berlin for the last time?

RV: In 1939, just a few hours before the Germans invaded Poland. I was warned. I had to leave secretly. I didn't take anything with me. I told my maid, I will return late. Go to bed. I never returned. She didn't know that I was leaving. I'd sent my wife and children out of the country earlier. My parents left with me. Everything you see here I acquired since 1941 when I came to this country.

JB: What about the negatives?

RV: I carried some with me, sewn into my clothes, and left some with my father in France, where he was in hiding from the Nazis with the help of a landlady. He kept them under the floor or behind paintings on the wall, wrapped in paper. Some of them suffered, naturally. But this was a time of terror, and it was dangerous to keep negatives.

JB: What kind of a reception did your photographs get in the United States?

RV: Nobody was interested. The Jewish organizations wanted to destroy the negatives. They thought that their relations did not look or act different from themselves. Suddenly, they were confronted with pictures of poor people, looking very different from them. So they were afraid. They considered me the greatest enemy. I had the most difficulties with the big Jewish organizations. I won't say which, because today the situation is changed, and the people in them are different. I'm not trying to take revenge. Times were different then.

JB: But Schocken Books published a collection of photographs in 1947.

RV: It was poorly done.

JB: Why did so many years elapse between that version and *A Vanished World*?

RV: I've had a contract since 1975, but the publisher didn't want to publish it until a few years ago. The salespeople said it would be impossible to sell. No one was interested in the past. Everyone wanted to see pretty girls and pleasant things. Now it is a bestseller.

JB: I'm curious about the two sets of captions that go with each photograph in the book. There are short ones with each photograph and longer, more descriptive ones in a section at the front of the book. The longer ones provide details that make looking at these photographs a truly heart-wrenching experience, but flipping back and forth is awkward, and even the longer captions left me wanting to know more.

RV: I wrote the stories. The publisher did not want them at all at first. Then a friend shortened them. They do not tell the whole story. They are too short. But what can you do? The publisher is the boss.

JB: Yet captions providing information about time and place are so essential to documentary photographs. A perfect example is the photograph taken on Kristallnacht [when the Nazis burned hundreds of Jewish homes, businesses, and synagogues, and murdered, tortured, or arrested thousands of Jews]. For one, since it's a close-up of a child's face, it would be impossible to know when it was taken without the caption. Another illuminating detail—in fact, a shocking detail—is that you were wearing a Nazi uniform that night.

RV: Yes. Some of the things I did to get the pictures were not easy, but I had to do it, or I would not have a picture. There was a whole store full of uniforms. When I bought it, they didn't check on me. They presumed I needed it. A Jew would never buy one.

JB: The little girl seems to be looking directly at the camera. Is she so terror-stricken because of the uniform?

RV: I don't think that she was afraid of me, because I was one of many. Maybe she saw a weapon. They were in a murderous state.

JB: Did you go back to Germany after the war?

RV: Yes, I returned in 1945. I still had hopes that I would find someone who had survived. But I did not find anything. That was the sad story.

JB: Have you heard from any of the people you photographed?

RV: Yes. I heard from one lady who lives in the Bronx. She's a grandmother now. She saw herself in the book and called me. There was a big excitement. It was right after the book came out, three years ago.

She was only eleven years old when I took her picture in 1938. Her parents, brother, and sister were murdered. She was the only one to survive.

JB: You often describe your life and survival as miraculous. Even before you moved to Berlin, during your years in Russia, you had a number of close calls. How did that affect your feelings about God?

RV: I am very religious. I go to synagogue because I like the ceremony. I belong to an Orthodox congregation. But I am a scientist. A scientist must be critical. There are a thousand religions, and everyone tells you his god is better than any other god. I believe in God, which is in human beings.

JB: Do you believe in a spiritual life after death?

RV: I think that life goes on in the relatives who remain.

JB: What sort of reception did *A Vanished World* receive in Israel?

RV: It was phenomenal. At the exhibition, I could hardly move. People wouldn't let me go. I had to stay all the time, from morning to evening. Even in the street, they embraced me, they kissed me, and they asked me millions of questions. It was really moving.

People understand that my book is of great importance because those depicted are no more. And they are important because of their goodness, their belief in goodness. That's religion.

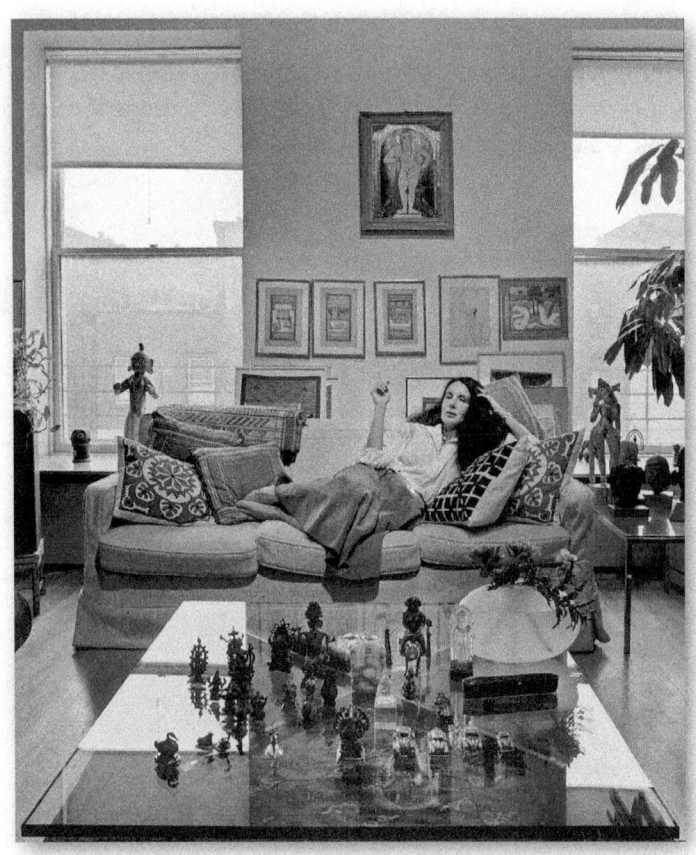

Photo by Kurt Fishback

MARY ELLEN MARK (1940–2015)

Street Shooter

Published January/February 1987

I t was the early sixties. Mary Ellen Mark was a graduate student, studying painting at the University of Pennsylvania. On a whim, she decided to take a course in photography. She picked up a Leica. Then she abandoned the brush forever and took to the streets. Mark earned a degree in photojournalism in 1964 and a year later won a Fulbright to photograph in Turkey. In 1969, she landed the assignment that established her reputation as a world-class photojournalist: *Look* sent her to London to photograph the city's teenage heroin addicts. The unforgettable images Mark brought back with her were just a harbinger of things to come.

Since that time, Mary Ellen Mark has undertaken just about every kind of assignment, both editorial and commercial. But she's at her best with the "tough" ones—going to India for *Paris-Match* to find youthful dropouts from Western civilization or photographing the best friend of a teen suicide for *Vanity Fair*.

Her most memorable work documents the lives of the dispossessed; those deprived by birth of the rights and amenities most of us take for granted touch her. When that happens, she virtually moves in with her subject. She spent thirty-six days in the maximum security section of the Oregon State Hospital, living with the mentally ill, for her 1979 book, *Ward 81*. And she spent three months with prostitutes in Bombay for her 1981 book, *Falkland Road*.

In 1983, *Life* sent Mark to Seattle for photographs of the child hustlers who inhabit its streets for lack of better homes. Afterward, she returned to

Seattle with her husband, documentary filmmaker Martin Bell. Seven months later, they had the raw footage for the film *Streetwise*.

Mark has a rare gift for engaging the trust of her subjects. They reveal themselves to her sympathetic lens to an often unsettling degree, sharing their most intimate moments, as well as rage and sorrow and brittle moments of happiness.

Home base for Mark is an airy loft in New York City. It overlooks one of the most fashionable intersections in SoHo, but that's just chance, since it was purchased when struggling artists and warehouses still predominated in this now posh neighborhood.

A table bisects one end of the long, open room, delineating office space where Mark's assistant answers phones on this gray workday morning. At the room's center, three worn couches, covered with Indian throws and pillows, form a horseshoe around a glass coffee table. It displays an assortment of miniatures made of spun and beaten silver. These are just a few of the room's reminders of Mark's affection for India.

It's here that we talk, as classical music plays softly. She never quite comes to rest. Though warm and open, she's clearly eager to be back at work.

JB: Given your original interest in painting, why did you choose photojournalism over a more formal approach to photography?

MEM: I just knew from the minute I picked up a camera that I wanted to photograph people and do social documentary photographs. I didn't really become a serious student until then. No one could understand my passion for photography. It came out of the blue. I was never a very technical person.

JB: You're best known for your documentaries of disadvantaged subcultures—projects like *Ward 81*, *Falkland Road*, and *Streetwise*. Why do you think you're drawn to such subjects?

MEM: I'm interested in people who haven't had all the lucky breaks in life—people who are handicapped emotionally, physically, or financially. Much of life is luck. No one can choose whether he's born into a wealthy, privileged home or born into extreme poverty. I guess I'm interested in people who haven't had as much of a chance because they reach out more, they need more. They touch me. I do a lot of other work to support myself, but those kinds of projects are the reasons I became a photographer.

JB: You began publishing in *Look*, *Life*, *Ms.*, *Paris-Match*, and *Esquire* in the late sixties, when there was a much greater demand for social documentary pictures. How have changes in the editorial market since then affected your work?

MEM: It's very difficult to interest magazines in long documentary essays these days. The magazines approach me mostly for portraits because that's mainly what they do now. I love to do those, too, if I can make a statement about the person. Magazines have gotten much more conservative. When I shot the street kids in Seattle for *Life*, there was a picture of a boy shooting up a girl, probably with MDA [3,4-Methylenedioxyamphetamine]. People were shocked by that photograph. But fifteen years ago, I did an essay for *Look* that was nothing but pictures of kids shooting up. It would be very difficult to publish an essay like that now. People accepted these realities then; now they don't. Look at how times have changed!

JB: Why is that?

MEM: In-depth stories take time, and they're expensive. Sometimes the pictures are harder to look at. Most magazines seem to want simple solutions—pictures that are easy to look at and don't pose any questions. There's so much of this slick, homogenized portraiture that's more about the photographer than the subject. And with this kind of portraiture, it's difficult to tell one photographer from another anymore. I like portraits that tell me something about the person being photographed, not how clever the photographer is because he got someone to jump in the air or stand on his head.

Do you want to know whose work I really admire? Helmut Newton. His portraits shake people up. The other day I picked up his little book of black-and-white portraits (*Helmut Newton: Portretten/Portraits*), and I thought, "These pictures take risks!" They tell you something about the person he's photographing.

JB: When you undertake documentary projects—and you immerse yourself in them, virtually living with your subjects for months at a time—how do you want people to respond to the pictures you take?

MEM: I want people to be moved by them.

JB: To the point where they want to change some of the conditions they see?

MEM: I'm not sure that photography changes anything, but I think it's important to recognize that runaway kids and women who survive by selling their bodies exist. Many people lead protected and sheltered lives, and I think it's important for them to look at other ways of life.

JB: You want to shake people's complacency?

MEM: Some people's complacency you can never shake, but yes.

JB: Some of your photographs are quite shocking. For example, the overhead shots of the Falkland Road prostitutes in bed with their customers. There's a scene in *Streetwise* where a street girl confronts her mother about being molested by her stepfather. Are your subjects sometimes as interested in rocking the boat as you are?

MEM: The girl in *Streetwise* definitely did want to rock the boat. She was aware we were there, and I think she said what she said because she wanted the world to be aware of her too. As for the prostitutes, that's just what they do. It's normal for them. They sell their bodies for money, and I thought it was important to show them working, because that's a real clue to their lives.

One thing's for sure: In the kind of social documentary photography I do, you're never a fly on the wall like you are when you photograph a disaster or a war, and the event is more important than your presence. You're as much a part of the scene as your subjects. They never forget you're there.

JB: When is it inappropriate to take a photograph? How do you know when you're violating a subject's trust?

MEM: All kinds of photography teach you to be exceptionally perceptive, but particularly social documentary photography, because you're so involved with your subjects. *Ward 81* taught me a lot about sensitivity. Those women had serious mental problems. That didn't mean they weren't sensitive. On the contrary, they were more sensitive. If you were aware, they would send you all kinds of signals about when you could and could not go near them. All people are like that. They send signals, and you have to know how far you can push in any given situation. But I also think it's very important to get strong and intimate photographs. You do have to push.

JB: Are you an outgoing person?

MEM: I'm actually not. I'm really shy. But I'm able to do what I have to do—I'm outgoing enough to be able to photograph. I don't think you can be terribly meek and do this kind of work. But making the initial contact is hard. It's like jumping into cold water.

JB: Do you get emotionally involved in your work?

MEM: Definitely.

JB: Do you make any attempt to maintain objectivity?

MEM: There's no such thing as being objective on a personal project. If you care about it, then you have to be subjective. But it's very easy to make pictures lie, so you have to be fair in that sense. When I was photographing *Falkland Road*, there was a scuffle between a madam and a girl. I shot some pictures, but when they were printed, I realized it looked as if the woman was beating the girl. She wasn't. It was half in fun, but it looked violent.

JB: Does your life become intertwined with your subjects?

MEM: It can't help but do that. If it's a great story, you're totally involved in it.

JB: What kind of toll does that take on you when it's time to say good-bye?

MEM: It does take a toll on you, and it's not something you ever forget. The people you've worked with, if they've meant something to you, are going to live with you forever. You also feel a tremendous amount of guilt because you've taken something from them. They've given you something great, and how can you ever repay them?

JB: Do you stay in touch?

MEM: I try to. We've really kept in touch with the kids in Seattle. We've received lots of collect telephone calls.

JB: Have your photographs, or the film, sparked any changes in your subjects' lives?

MEM: I wish I could say yes, especially with the kids. But they had many painful years before we met them. When you're working with them, you say all the right things: "You're stupid to sell your body. You're stupid to steal. Why don't you try to make something of your life? You're bright." Whether the kids want to listen is another thing. I think contact with us showed them there are alternatives, but it's too soon to tell how that will affect them. I keep hoping someone will adopt Tiny [one of the girls in the film], but that's a dream and life isn't like that.

JB: What was your own childhood like?

MEM: Pretty normal. I was head cheerleader in high school. I grew up in Philadelphia. My father was a builder—he died when I was a teenager. My mother didn't work. I have a half brother, but he was much older than me, so I was raised as an only child. I grew up knowing that I wanted to do something, to be independent.

JB: How do you fit marriage and a family life into a career like yours?

MEM: I made the decision not to have children a long time ago. In this kind of work, it's hard to have kids. I never thought I would get married, but then I met Martin. He's been very inspiring and supportive about my work, and I hope he feels the same way about me. We have similar interests and work styles. We're both interested in documentary subjects. We argued as all people do while we were making *Streetwise*, but we never disagreed for a moment about the point of view of the film. We're both very wrapped up in our work. It's totally consuming, and it's good to be with someone who understands that. We both travel a lot, but it's no problem. If something comes up I just go, and the same with him.

JB: How much is a lot?

MEM: Let me tell you about my summer. In May, I worked on *A Day in the Life of America*. Then I went to Miami, and I shot an album cover for Don Johnson. After that, I spent three weeks in Hong Kong and a few days in Korea for the *London Sunday Times Magazine*. From there, I went to Carmel to teach a Friends of Photography workshop. I came back to New York, and the *London Sunday Times* called again. I flew to Hawaii for them to photograph Marcos. I came back to New York, and then I went to Aspen to teach another workshop. From there, I flew to Idaho to photograph a meeting of the Aryan

Nations—an extreme rightwing group. After that, I taught in Maine for a week. I came back to New York and decided I was going to relax. But *Life* called, wanting me to go immediately to Pakistan, so I did. After that, I went to Toronto to work on a film.

Between Martin and me, we've accumulated all these free airline tickets from collecting mileage. I've got to figure out how to use them.

JB: Take a vacation?

MEM: [Laughing] I haven't had a vacation in years.

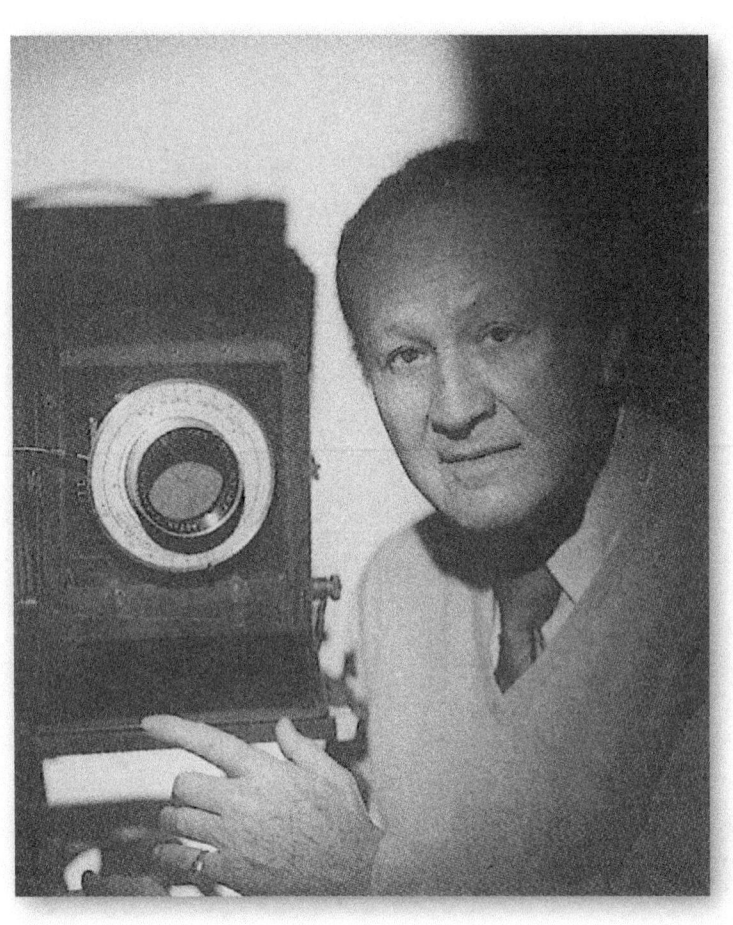

JAMES J. KRIEGSMANN (1909–1994)

An Eye for Entertainers

Published March/April 1987

Start at the intersection of Broadway and Forty-Second Street—New York City's Time Square. Head north up Broadway, the Great White Way, named before the now-prevailing neon, when just white lights illuminated the area's outsized billboards and theater marquees. At Forty-Sixth Street, turn east. There, just steps from the garish hub of the theater district, is a plain, beige storefront studio with a large, stylized signature above the door. No bright lights are needed here, for just about everyone in show biz knows the name, James J. Kriegsmann. The spiky signature logo, faintly old fashioned, is all the advertisement that's needed now. His business? Theatrical photography.

There's a lot of entertainment history—and more—behind this modest façade. Since 1935, when Kriegsmann opened his first studio here, he has photographed burlesque queens, movie stars, nightclub entertainers, even politicians. Many of his clients were popular musicians. In the 1984 book by Michael Ochs, *Rock Archives,* a rock 'n' roll history in photographs, no one's credit line appears more often than Kriegsmann's. He was one of the original rock photographers, shooting pop stars in the early days of rock 'n' roll, when most hits songs were still just good, clean fun. Kriegsmann's pictures were clean compositions, too, as tightly choreographed as a Motown Review—all sequins, satin, and glamor spotlighting.

They were pretty pictures, slick publicity stills destined to illustrate some bit of theatrical news on the entertainment pages or to be showcased in theater lobbies, scribbled across and mailed to fans, and tacked to deli walls. Today, these pictures represent not only a bygone era but also the sheer talent of the man whose job it was to elevate from the ordinary to the sublime those who came to him.

Kriegsmann arrived from Austria with his widowed father, his brother, and his two sisters only days before the stock market crashed in 1929. He was just twenty. In Vienna, he had worked as a photographer's apprentice, starting by cleaning toilets, then learning to process film, make and retouch prints, and, finally, to photograph. It was a standard, three-year routine, culminating in a studio exam.

Intending to eventually make his way to Hollywood (he never did) after settling in New York, Kriegsmann parlayed his skills into a job as a retoucher at Strand Studios, whose clients were primarily burlesque emporiums. "We didn't have such things in Vienna," asserts Kriegsmann, who, along with the film, was thus exposed to a lot of bare flesh.

At seventy-seven, he no longer does the photography, unless someone is willing to pay his personal fee of $1,000. He'd rather oversee the still-flourishing business—his is the oldest such studio in Manhattan—and leave the shooting to his sons, Jimmy Jr. and Tommy. Examples of his sons' work—portraits of men and women with flawless features and a subtle glow of self-assurance—ring the street-level reception area.

Only one of the elder Kriegsmann's photographs now hangs there, one of Cab Calloway, made when Kriegsmann was the official photographer for the Cotton Club Review, soon after it opened, two blocks to the North. With shameless hyperbole, the Cotton Club had billed him as the "famous Viennese photographer" though he had never been more than a photographer's assistant in Vienna, and at the time had been in business for himself for only a few years.

Celebrity Focus

It's difficult to think of a celebrity who hasn't been flattered by Kriegsmann's camera. He photographed Frank Sinatra, Pat Boone, and Buddy Holly, among others. Johnny Carson and Joan Rivers sat for him long before their late-night shows. His glamorous photographs aided the ascent of many Motown stars, including the Temptations, the Miracles, and the Supremes.

Politicians came too. Nelson Rockefeller's favorite portrait was a Kriegsmann. "He gave me a great compliment once. He walked in and said, 'I have never in my life seen a studio like this!'" recounts Kriegsmann.

Having visited the Kriegsmann studio, it's easy to understand Rockefeller's reaction. For the past thirty years, the studio has occupied the large basement space that was once Zimmerman's, a Hungarian nightclub and restaurant. When he moved in, Kriegsmann kept several of the restaurant's features, adapting them to his own purposes. A wide, curving staircase, ideal for regal entrances, leads down into the studio proper. Tucked under the stairs is a full-fledged bar and a handful of little tables covered with checked tablecloths. A mural of a party of poker-playing dogs, barely discernible in the indirect lighting from desk lamps, decorates the wall above vintage banquettes.

To the left, through a doorway, stand two grand pianos, favorite Kriegsmann props. Sinatra liked the white one. Beyond are makeup stations, shooting spaces, color and black-and-white darkrooms, and printing facilities (Kriegsmann began mass processing of photographs during World War II, printing large quantities of war-zone scenes for the government in exchange for a guaranteed supply of hard-to-get paper and chemicals.) From somewhere indeterminate, strobes flash and Top 40 music plays.

Kriegsmann says he left the bar intact because "it's part of our business. Performers come, and sometimes they're nervous. They need a little bit of a lift." He tells a story of a pair of comedians who requested a pricey brand of liquor, which they sipped throughout their session. When presented with the bill for the photography, which included a charge for the liquor, they were aghast. Says Kriegsmann, "They said, "Even the Cotton Club doesn't charge *this* much for a bottle!"

Kriegsmann speaks with the ease and cadences of one who has been interviewed often. No need to question him. He's ready with a series of anecdotes well tested for entertainment value, each introducing the next. "I used to get a tremendous amount of publicity," he says. "I was on every television show and every radio talk show."

The Importance of Being Frank

Kriegsmann's most fertile source of anecdotes is Frank Sinatra, whom he photographed repeatedly throughout the singer's early career. However, he is clearly ambivalent about Sinatra; a clash of wills eventually ended the mutually advantageous relationship. "To me," he says, "Frank Sinatra is an enigma. The man is unbelievable. Even now, with his potbelly and hair plants, he is a great, great artist. I benefited an awful lot, being associated with Frankie. No question."

And Sinatra had the advantage of Kriegsmann's instinct for publicity when the singer was still unknown and, as Kriegsmann tells it, still unpolished. "The first time, he came in wearing a tuxedo with no cuffs. I said, 'Frankie, you can't wear a tuxedo with no cuffs!' So I got out some tissue paper and made him some cuffs."

Just before the singer's first smash solo performance at New York's Paramount Theatre, his publicity man came to Kriegsmann. "'Jimmy,' he said, 'this kid has got something. We've got to do something a little bit different.' Well, those were the years when every performer wore a tuxedo or tails." Instead, Kriegsmann dressed Sinatra in a sport coat and bow tie, and combed his hair loose, with one curl hanging over his forehead—a look that became Sinatra's trademark. The picture topped the Paramount marquee throughout Sinatra's engagement.

"At first I didn't think Sinatra was that good," Kriegsmann remembers of the man who took to practicing at the white piano in the then fourth-floor studio. "Then I took my wife to see him. I was flabbergasted! He had personality!"

During World War II, it was Kriegsmann's idea to photograph Sinatra at the piano, holding his tiny daughter, Nancy. The purpose: To remind the public that Sinatra was a father, and thus exempt from the draft.

Makeup and Lighting

Kriegsmann was uniquely skilled at painting his subjects in the best possible light, literally and figuratively. Some performers needed little help on this score. Johnny Carson, for example, had "a perfect face." Others needed corrective measures. When Sinatra was too poor to pay Kriegsmann, let alone have his teeth fixed, Kriegsmann retouched them. And he obscured the less photogenic side of the singer's face by casting it in shadow.

Then there were the Andrews Sisters. Six years ago, *Esquire* quoted Kriegsmann as saying, "They sure were ugly girls." The picture captioned with that remark belies the statement, and Kriegsmann says he was misunderstood. He points to one of the sisters. "I made her chin a little longer; I gave her a beautiful nose. I gave her lips and cheekbones. All with makeup. But they were not bad looking. As far as I'm concerned, there is no such thing as an ugly person."

In general, he disliked retouching. It was time-consuming, and it sometimes showed. He preferred to make alterations with makeup and lighting, before exposing the negative. "I would always try to improve appearance," says Kriegsmann, who thus filled in hairlines, shaved jowls, sculpted noses and shaped cheekbones. "Every nose has to have a bridge," he advises.

Like most theatrical photographers of his day, Kriegsmann worked with an 8 x 10 view camera. He especially liked his Deardorff, which he would adjust to lengthen a short face or to shorten a long one. In his profession, such tricks were *de rigueur.*

Kriegsmann's groupings and his static renditions of classic nightclub staging were distinctive. So, too, was his lighting, which he says he learned by watching three or four movies a week. I very seldom missed a new motion picture. I used to sit down and just look at the lighting. Then I copied it."

He used incandescent lights, never flash. He says he never used a light meter and often didn't even bother to check the image on the ground glass, relying on instinct to tell him when the setup was perfect. He would make a few blank shots to relax the subject before he actually started exposing film.

The Big Break
Kriegsmann's first big break involved the Flying Wallendas, one of the great circus aerial acts. It happened while he was still working at Strand Studios.

When the circus came to town, the Wallendas showed up at Strand to have their pictures taken. Kriegsmann, though still an apprentice, won the assignment by default, because the aerialists spoke only German, and he was the only staff member who could communicate with them.

So began a lifelong friendship and the steady expansion of his clientele, as the Wallendas sent other circus performers to him. But the contact briefly dimmed his interest in photography. He became obsessed with their lives and ways and decided to join the circus himself. Carl Wallenda dissuaded him, saying, "You dammed fool! Don't do it!"

Before long, Kriegsmann left Strand and opened his own place, which he called Studio One. By the time the Cotton Club made him its official photographer, he had honed his technique to a fine edge and had built a solid reputation. Photographing black faces was a new challenge. Kriegsmann still bridles at the memory of warnings that photographing blacks would irreparably damage his career. "I said, 'Don't tell me that! They're human beings like you and me. Sure, their skin may be different. But the talent they have, most of the white people haven't got. That's the truth.'"

Musical Interlude

Whether they were black or white, Kriegsmann found inspiration in the musicians he photographed. Around 1953, he began writing music. "I love music," he says. "I studied the violin. I absorbed so much music in Vienna and from all the activity here in New York that I could sit down and write without any problem. Only music. Not lyrics."

He took an office on the third floor of the Brill Building, sharing it with two songwriting partners. This became Studio Two. Studio One remained open for photo business while he and his two partners composed music. One of their songs, "Joey," hit number eleven on the charts. "Almost the Top Ten," says Kriegsmann. And Mantovani recorded their tango, "Desiree." "It did very well in the South American countries, but those were the years here when they didn't plan many instrumentals. Mostly vocals. Finally, we had a hit with 'The Happy Organ,' recorded by Dave 'Baby' Cortez in 1959. At that time, the disc jockeys took graft. We picked three spots—Buffalo, Baltimore, and Chicago. We paid them each $150. Now that's illegal. Then it wasn't. About a week later, we got calls from all three of them. 'You've got a hit! A *big* hit!'

"We were number one for two solid weeks across the country. We made so much money, we went crazy! Even today I get royalties. Not much. I couldn't live on it. But it's enough to buy me pretzels every day."

Fighting Words

Kriegsmann also became a professional writer. For a time he wrote a column called "World in Focus," purchasing space in the *New York Herald Tribune* to publish it. Big business and Walter Winchell, the famous columnist and radio newscaster (and a Kriegsmann photo subject) were the impetus. It served as a steam valve as well as a clever self-promotion.

He began writing it in the late thirties, when the government froze prices. Like many small businessmen, Kriegsmann was caught off guard. But some large firms, he remembers, raised their prices just weeks before the freeze. "I was angry. I thought, 'Why can't I write my political views, like Walter Winchell does?'"

He did just that, starting with an editorial deploring government favoritism toward big business at the expense of the little guy. "I got so much mail you wouldn't believe it!" After that, he published the column every Monday until the day before Eisenhower's election to the presidency. He signed off with early congratulations to the candidate he had championed.

But songwriting and editorializing, for all their rewards, were never more than peripheral enterprises. Photography was central to Kriegsmann's life. And the studio became a family business. "Did you see the beautiful redhead upstairs when you came in?" he asks. "That's my wife." Kriegsmann met her when she came in looking for a modeling job, at age seventeen. They've been married for forty-three years.

Only one son has flown the Kriegsmann coop, a broker who lives in Seattle; the other two stayed with the business. Their growing interest in photography dovetailed neatly with his own retreat from the camera, coming along as the stagey, large-format portraits that were his specialty began losing favor to more candid small-format stills. The involvement of his sons, using a more up-to-date approach, allowed the studio to stay in business while many of Kriegsmann's contemporaries faded from the scene.

In the end, there's one last tale to tell before heading upstairs and out. "This famous comedian—what was his name?—brought me a grandfather clock. He left it here." Kriegsmann points to the middle of the room. "It was *ugly*. When he went into makeup, I picked it up to move it out of sight. He came running out with this big grin on his face. He said, 'Jimmy, you shouldn't be carrying that thing around like that! It's heavy. You should really get a wristwatch.'"

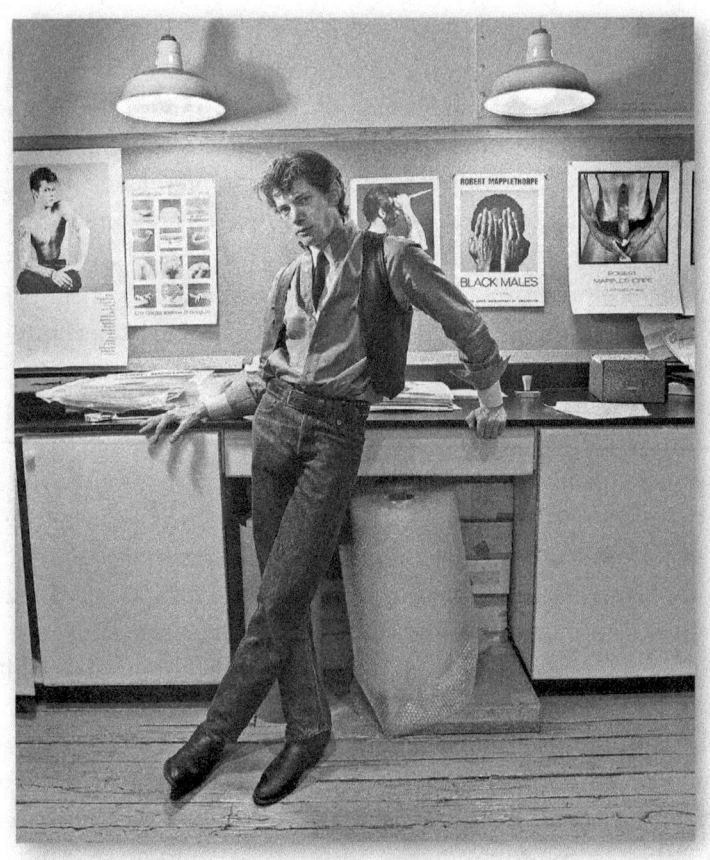

Photo by Kurt Fishback

Bad Boy Makes Good

Published July/August 1988

There are signs of encroaching prosperity on New York City's Bond Street. Crumbling tenements crisscrossed with rusting fire escapes shoulder up to once-industrial loft buildings in various stages of renovation. For years, dance studios, parking lots, storefront theater groups, and struggling artists quietly coexisted in this fringe neighborhood. But these days, drifters from the nearby Bowery missions share the sidewalk with well-healed speculators, drawn to the street because of its closeness to trendy SoHo, a few blocks South.

"Mapplethorpe" reads the nameplate next to a steel door on a tenement as yet untouched by progress. Photographer Robert Mapplethorpe used to live here. Now, he lives on Twenty-Third Street but maintains this Bond Street address to attend to business and meet with clients, curators, and reporters. For Mapplethorpe, fortune was slow to follow the fame he achieved in the early seventies when his pictures of underground sexuality shocked the art world. But for him too, prosperity has at long last arrived.

One of Mapplethorpe's three assistants descends in the rattling freight elevator that takes us up to a long, dim loft. The low light here transforms everything to tones of black-and-white. Mapplethorpe, usually sighted wearing black, is out of uniform. Today, he's dressed in neutral tones. Gone is the skull jewelry reporters unfailingly noted a few years back. There's also no sign of the photographs that launched his notoriety and, with his visible membership in the nocturnal downtown demimonde, caused the media to dub him "the bad boy of photography."

That image is fading, mellowing with time and hard-won success. At forty-one, Mapplethorpe is acclaimed as one of the most outstanding artists of his generation. He's a current favorite of purveyors of both art and commercial photography. He exhibits continually around the world, and his last New York show, at Robert Miller Gallery, sold out. He takes as many commercial assignments as he can handle. "I'm really proud of the stuff I do commercially," he says. He's generally given creative license, and it's not hard to recognize his signature style on ads and editorial pages in *Vanity Fair, Interview, Stern, Vogue,* and *House & Garden.* Rose's Lime Juice recruited him for its latest ad campaign. This time, he appears on the other side of the camera. Paired with photographer Norman Parkinson, who represents a traditional/conservative talent, Mapplethorpe represents the downtown artist who has achieved an uptown success.

Working in black-and-white, Mapplethorpe has consistently explored three broad subjects—nudes, portraits, and still lifes—rendering each with the technical perfection that is his hallmark. Drawn to the shadows more than to the light, he focuses on secret, dark, and dangerous qualities. His images are almost always still, frozen in time. Nothing moves. He likes to give his pictures an "edge"—even his flowers. He told an interviewer earlier this year, "Some of [the flowers] have a sort of sinister side…a certain edge, a creepy quality."

Mapplethorpe's talent has always had its champions; John McKendry at the Metropolitan Museum of Art was an early mentor. But many pundits were slow to find words of praise. The nudes, which dared to illustrate sexual/social taboos and a more than documentary fascination with them, triggered moral outrage in many viewers. Critics found much to revile in his pornographic Polaroids: studies of the S-and-M scene and heterosexual and homosexual couples engaged in sexual acts. His pictures of nude black men, published in one of his books, *Black Males: Power and Beauty,* sparked angry accusations that he was promoting destructive racial stereotypes. "Man in a Polyester Suit, 1980," the torso of a dressed black male with his penis showing, has become the best known among these. Declaimers called his work tasteless and exploitative. In 1983, *The New York Times* described an exhibit as "undeniably and intentionally distasteful…chic, narcissistic exhibitionism."

Mapplethorpe says he was unprepared for such vehement criticism. He claims he chose his subjects because he found them attractive. Exploitation was neither intended by him nor perceived by them. He just wanted to make pictures that had never been done before. "Nobody with a real aesthetic had ever gone into that area. I thought people's eyes would be opened, because I always showed them in conjunction with the other pictures. I'd have a picture of fruit or flowers next to a picture of sexuality next to a portrait of someone socially prominent. My intent was to open people's eyes, get them to realize anything can be acceptable. It's not what it is; it's the way it's photographed. But it made people hate the flowers and hate the people in the pictures. I didn't intend that at all."

Still, Mapplethorpe did not stop showing erotic themes, and that made some wonder if he was purposefully choosing controversial subjects that would ensure he would be remembered. Mapplethorpe denies it. What about his bad-boy image? Is it an image that appeals to him? "Not really. It's cute. I've done exactly what I wanted to do, and if that's being bad..." He trails off.

But he did little to discourage the bad-boy image. For interviews, he always dressed in black. He talked incessantly about sex. In self-portraits that invite speculation about his personal life, he poses in lipstick and makeup, wearing a black leather jacket and toting a machine gun, as a devil with horns and a demon with a whiptail. Why the getup? "Oh, just something to do," says Mapplethorpe now. "Periodically, I have a show and people want pictures of me, so I just do a self-portrait. It's as simple as that. I don't like to repeat myself. I try to come up with some kind of gimmick that I think is interesting."

Mapplethorpe tells interviewers about his distaste for light, mentioning that when he lived with rock poet Patti Smith at the Chelsea Hotel, he had a back section with no window, where it was completely dark. "You didn't know what time of day it was. I can live that way." Bruce Chatwin's preface to Mapplethorpe's 1983 book *Lady*, featuring bodybuilder Lisa Lyon, refers to Mapplethorpe's "night-biased" world. Is he still a night person? "At one time more than now," he says mildly. "I basically stay up late and get up late."

What's known about Mapplethorpe is only partially illuminating. He grew up in Floral Park, Long Island, and studied painting and sculpture at the Pratt Institute in Brooklyn. Raised as a Catholic, he says the church definitely influenced his work and claims to have an abiding fascination with Catholic ritual. When he left Pratt, he moved in with Smith and lived with her for seven years.

These days he's not inclined to elaborate on his past. Anyone who wants to know him can simply study his photographs; his work, he says, "is quite autobiographical. I'm pretty honest and I think the pictures say a lot about me. The experience is more important than the photograph."

Mapplethorpe likes to photograph those with whom he most enjoys spending his time. For him, the photo session itself is on a par with the finished image. Although he has taken beautiful portraits of children, he quickly admits they're not his favorite subjects. When working in portraiture, Mapplethorpe's preferred subjects are celebrities. He says he's just not inspired by "plain people." They don't interest him, perhaps because he already knows what they're like. He grew up with and away from plain people, he says.

During a sitting with an inspiring subject, Mapplethorpe says a kind of magic takes place—a spark that ignites a powerful communion between photographer and subject. In 1983, he told the British magazine *The Face* that it was "sort of abstract and parallel to drugs where you lose yourself in this relationship between the subject and the self."

The portraits, usually undertaken as editorial projects, are slow to sell. Among his imagery, the bestsellers are his still lifes, especially the flowers, which are favorites among corporate buyers. The "edge" to these still lifes may come from the fact that he doesn't like flowers. But once he starts, he can get excited about photographing them, he says.

Mapplethorpe has published several books, including *Certain People: A Book of Portraits* and *Black Males: Power and Beauty. Lady,* which for Mapplethorpe represents a rare focus on the female form, was conceived as a commercial venture at a time when his finances were shaky. Photo books are rarely bestsellers. The project just barely broke even.

While his choice of subjects speak of his preoccupations at different times of his life, the technical precision of his prints and his faithfulness to black-and-white is also revealing. Whether he's photographing flowers, faces, or phalluses, Mapplethorpe's pictures share an uncommon obsession with every detail of composition and printing.

For several years, much of the task of printing has fallen to Tom Baril. He prints black-and-white silver images for Mapplethorpe and knows that the artist is a fanatic about all the lights, shadows, hot spots, and every possible detail being revealed in the print. Baril describes the printing process as standard and archival, with few darkroom tricks beyond perhaps diffusing the images through a sheet of frosted glass placed under the enlarger.

Mapplethorpe's black-and-white work is shot on Kodak T-Max 100 and developed in D-76 or FG-7. Baril feels that the FG-7 gives a somewhat better grain structure. All of the black-and-white prints are made in a custom darkroom equipped with an Omega D-5 enlarger, an Aristo cold-light head, and Rodagon lenses. The majority of his prints are made on Kodak Polyfiber paper N surface, with darker-skinned subjects printed on Agfa Portriga 118 matte surface. The paper is developed in Kodak Ektaflo developer and fixed and washed using Heico fix and washing aid. All black-and-white prints are toned in selenium for appearance and permanence.

Mapplethorpe admits to being a perfectionist. "I take a whole roll of the same image. Placement and cropping are really important. I don't want anything out of place. That's the way I am about how I arrange things where I live, too. I would like to think everything is perfect. I'm not somebody who takes photographs about chance. I'm not a street photographer. I couldn't be further removed." He usually shoots with a Halleslblad equipped with 120mm or 150mm lenses and sometimes with a Linhof. Most of his work is done in a studio and rarely with natural light. He is a minimalist.

Black-and-white preempted his attention for years both because it is relatively inexpensive and infinitely easier to control than color. Now that he can afford it, he has dye transfer prints made for his color work. They're expensive but allow him greater control for changing or correcting color. His foray into color is one of several ways in which the artist has been presenting himself with new challenges that are more aesthetic and technical than subjective. These also include experiments with oversized photogravures and platinum printing on canvas, linen, and silk. "I want to see something I've never seen before," he says.

Mapplethorpe also designs furniture and stage sets as well as the frames in which his photographs are exhibited in New York. "I never intended to be a photographer," he says. "I was just interested in making a statement about the time I was living in." He picked up a camera when he found that he couldn't sit still long enough to paint representational imagery. "I was interested in using photography to make an art statement, and I set out to use it in a way that it had never been used before."

At first, Mapplethorpe developed his style unencumbered by influences. He did not study photography in school and believes his initial ignorance of his predecessors worked to his advantage. "The first Polaroids I ever took—there's a style there. It's my own. I think one of the problems a lot of people have is that they see too much and they know too much. They never really see for themselves."

His friendship with John McKendry inspired him to begin looking at the work of other photographers, and he began amassing his own collection after meeting Sam Wagstaff in 1973. Both men undertook to educate themselves in the history of photography together. "I just started taking pictures, developed a way of looking, and then started looking at the history of photography. I think that of all the photographers who've existed, certainly in this century, Man Ray is the most important because he kicked around photography in a way that hadn't been done before. He was more than a photographer. He and the portrait photographer Nadar influence my work in a subconscious way. But I think in the end I came up with a signature that's my own."

"Coming of age during the pop-art movement also had its effect," he concurs. He says he approaches his subjects and the making of art in general without prejudice.

Mapplethorpe has long been a celebrity in his own right, at least in New York City. As his fame spreads, and sales accrue, his image is softening. It might be the cautious orchestration of a new upscale image. As he says, he likes to be in control, likes everything to be perfect. But then too, time mellows us. We grow out of certain obsessions. The fast pace of youth slows naturally—helped in the eighties by fear of AIDS. It has affected his work subconsciously, Mapplethorpe says. "The kinds of pictures I took in the seventies I wouldn't take today, because of AIDS and also because I've done them already."

Whatever the motive, or lack of one, for his reserve today, the outcome is the same: our attention is deflected from the man to his work. That's where he wants it. Rightfully so.

ABOUT THE AUTHOR

A graduate of the Iowa Writers' Workshop and recipient of a New Jersey Arts Council Fellowship for fiction, Janis Bultman was a Contributing Editor for *Darkroom Photography* magazine from 1981 until 1988. Her work has appeared in *Forbes,* Rolling Stone Press, *Photo District News, American Photographer, Super-8 Filmaker, Moving Image, Arts Metro, Buddy, The Sun, San Jose Studies, Pacific Review, Belltrist Review,* and *Eureka Literary Magazine.* Bultman was raised in San Jose, California, and has lived in Berkeley, Los Angeles, New York, Chicago, New Jersey, London, and Portland, Oregon. She now lives in Iowa and teaches English at Kirkwood Community College in Cedar Rapids.